The
Way of
Mystery

The Way of Mystery

THE EUCHARIST AND MORAL LIVING

Dennis J. Billy, CSsR, and James Keating
Foreword by Lawrence S. Cunningham

Paulist Press
New York/Mahwah, N.J.

The Scripture quotations contained herein are from the New Revised Standard Version: Catholic Edition Copyright © 1989 and 1993, by the Division of Christian Education of the National Council of the Churches of Christ in the United States of America. Used by permission. All rights reserved.

Excerpts from the English translation of *The Roman Missal* © 1973, International Committee on English in the Liturgy, Inc. All rights reserved.

Cover and book design by Lynn Else
Cover photograph by Nancy de Flon

Library of Congress Cataloging-in-Publication Data

Billy, Dennis Joseph.
    The way of mystery : the Eucharist and moral living / Dennis J. Billy and James Keating ; foreword by Lawrence S. Cunningham.
        p. cm.
    Includes bibliographical references.
    ISBN 0-8091-4377-1 (alk. paper)
    1. Lord's Supper—Catholic Church. 2. Spiritual life—Catholic Church. 3. Catholic Church—Doctrines. I. Keating, James. II. Title.
    BX2215.3.B55 2006
    234'.163—dc22

                                                    2005026711

Published by Paulist Press
997 Macarthur Boulevard
Mahwah, New Jersey 07430

www.paulistpress.com

Printed and bound in the
United States of America

Contents

Dedication:

To the Redemptorist and Redemptoristine communities
at Esopus, New York, in gratitude for their friendship,
encouragement, and prayerful support.
D.B.

To Marianne, in gratitude for twenty years of love
and commitment in Christ.
J.K.

—w—

Acknowledgment

We would like to gratefully acknowledge the excellent and generous editorial work of Elizabeth Palmer, MDiv, research assistant in the School of Theology at the Pontifical College Josephinum, in the production of this book.

Foreword

In the prologue to his third-century commentary on the Song of Songs, Origen of Alexandria notes that Solomon, who had received the gift of wisdom from God, wrote three books that are enshrined in the canonical scriptures: Proverbs, Ecclesiastes, and the Song of Songs. Origen "reads" those three books as putting a person on the road to Christian perfection. In Proverbs, a person learns to recognize vice and virtue, avoiding the former and embracing the latter. At this stage we are in the world of *ethike*—ethics. By embracing Ecclesiastes, a person now living the life of virtue sees the world of creation in a new fashion, detecting in it the presence of God. This is the stage of *theoria* or contemplation. Finally, with renewed sight one can approach the hidden meaning of the Song of Songs, which makes one able to speak to God, which is *theologia*.

This triad, made famous by Origen, goes through various permutations in the history of Christian spirituality and gives us, for example, the classic stages of purification, illumination, and union described variously by different spiritual writers. Saint Bonaventure, to cite one example from many, links the three stages of the spiritual life to the monastic practice of *lectio*: meditation brings peace; illumination in prayer brings the splendor of truth; and contemplation issues forth in the perfection of love. Other writers will ascribe other emphases to the threefold path, but the number and the description have remained canonical over the ages. About this triadic path in general, however, a number of observations can be made.

First, the "stages" of the spiritual life must not be conceived of in any static or linear fashion. That is, one must not think that one passes through the stage of purgation and then can leave it behind once illumination has been attained. Even great saints and mystics like John of the Cross would be the first to say that in their unitive experiences they still regard themselves as sinners who must cooperate with the purifying and elevating grace of God. When the great saints say that they are great sinners, they are not being merely rhetorical. The very word *stages* (or *ladders* or *mountain ascents,* and so on) has often misled people into forgetting that the spiritual life is symbiotic and dynamic rather than a mechanical plodding up to "perfection" by steps that need not be retraced. Nor should the parsing out of the following of these stages be a matter of preoccupation. Thomas Merton has wisely noted that people ought to stop constantly worrying about whether they are on the cusp of union.

Second, and more important, this journey of the spiritual life must not be conceived of as a solitary and individual effort detached from the Christian community. "Alone with the Alone" may make sense in the philosophical world of Plotinus but not in the Christian world. It is worthwhile remembering that the medieval hermits referred to their retreats as an *ecclesiola*—a little church. All Christians must stand accountable for their Christian lives, but the measure of those lives is never something done independent of a believing community. After all, we are instructed to say "Our" Father, not "My" Father.

The precise merit of Billy and Keating's book is that they triangulate the spiritual path with the lateral lines of the eucharistic life of the believing and worshiping community and concern with Christian moral development. The net result of their approach is that they provide a rich account of how people live within the church's liturgical life and, further, how that kind of life provides a theological grounding for ethics. To put the matter somewhat differently: these authors do not conceive of the path of spiritual perfection apart from the nourishment of the sacramental life of the church. Saint Thomas Aquinas calls the Eucharist the nourishment of pilgrims—*esca viatorum*—and the moral life that flows from (and is, paradoxically, anterior to) that same spiritual path.

By providing the rich matrix of sacramentality for the spiritual life, these authors provide an alternative to one unhappy trend in popular spirituality, namely, a kind of self-indulgent narcissism in which spirituality gets reduced to playing psychological games or becomes a therapeutic nostrum to assuage certain middle-class anxieties. There is too much of that sort of thing abroad. In fact, in the concluding pages of their book our authors argue that the depths of the Christian spiritual experience push a person not to the self alone but to others in a kind of letting go of the self. They have the teaching of the great spiritual masters and mistresses on their side on this point. After Teresa of Avila finishes her wonderful treatise on contemplative prayer in *The Interior Castle*, she asks if there are any criteria by which one can judge if one has entered into the seventh mansion of the castle. Her answer is—so typical of the blunt and earthy mistress of the mystical way—simple: the test is, does that person love her neighbor more? Teresa echoes the sentiments of the fourteenth-century mystic Meister Eckhart, who once told his Dominican confreres that were a person elevated into the ecstasy of Saint Paul's third heaven and a sick brother needed soup the more perfect thing would be to administer the soup.

This volume, then, is anything but spirituality "lite." It stays close to the liturgy of the church, keeps its gaze on the paschal mystery revealed in the scriptures, sees the human person as irreducibly social, and proposes a teleology that is both proximate (living in this real messy world) and final (to be drawn toward God). In the final analysis, this work is an attempt to heal the breach between spirituality and theology that, decades ago, Hans Urs von Balthasar singled out as one of the great tragedies of contemporary theology. May this book, then, be not only an example of how to marry solid theology and spirituality but a goad for others to do the same.

Lawrence S. Cunningham
John A. O'Brien Professor of Theology
The University of Notre Dame

Introduction

Scripture tells us that the earliest Christians referred to their newborn faith as "The Way" (Acts 9:2, 16:17). It also tells us that "they devoted themselves to the apostles' instruction and the common life, to the breaking of the bread and the prayers" (Acts 2:42). For these early Christians, the Eucharist was a central and dynamic force in their way of life. Breaking bread together crystallized their understanding of what it meant to be a follower of Christ and inspired them to proclaim his message to others. This act of common worship reminded them of the origins of their faith and propelled them onward to their grace-filled destiny. It looked both backward and forward in time and ushered Christ and his kingdom dramatically into their midst. The Eucharist, for these early Christians, was a source of great strength, yet a sign of suffering and contradiction. It was an act of thanksgiving and a way of mystery. It put them in contact with the passion and death of their Lord and laid out before them the path to glory.

Our purpose in this book is to plumb the depths of the eucharistic mystery and to uncover its significance for Christian life today. We seek to discover what implications the simple act of breaking bread together has for the concrete decisions Christians make in their daily lives. The Eucharist, we believe, must help Christians make their choices by discerning out of Christ's paschal mystery. For this process to take place, however, Christians must first understand how the Eucharist puts them in touch with Christ's passion, death, and resurrection, and what concrete implications being in touch with this mystery has for their lives. If Christian worship is to enliven the believing community, it must help the faithful to integrate the spiritual and moral dimensions of their lives by leading them to embrace the attitudes and values embraced by Christ. When seen in this light, the purpose of Christ's eucharistic action is to shape the minds and hearts of those gathered and empower them to reveal the presence of God's love in the warp and woof of daily life.

We develop our thought in five closely related chapters, each of which builds on the insights of what precedes it. In chapter 1, "The Paschal Mystery," we look at the meaning of Christ's passion, death, and resurrection for human existence. We highlight the mystery of the Easter event and show how it heals humanity of its deep inner wound so that it can share in the intimate friendship of God. In chapter 2, "The Paschal Mystery in the Eucharistic Liturgy," we discuss the relationship between the Easter event and the public worship of the church, with special emphasis on the Eucharist. There we describe how the Mass mediates Christ's paschal mystery to the believing community and enables it to worship the Father in Spirit and in truth. In chapter 3, "The Eucharist as Source for Moral Formation," we examine the moral relevance of the paschal mystery by demonstrating how the eucharistic liturgy presents the believing community with the call to ongoing conversion. In this chapter, we assert that the Eucharist holds a central place in conscience formation, because Christ's paschal mystery unfolds within the believing community and engages it during the Liturgy of the Word and the Liturgy of the Eucharist. In chapter 4, "The Three Ways, Liturgy, and Moral Living," we explain how the Eucharist uses an ongoing process of purgation-illumination-union to shape the spiritual and moral life of the believing community. When the body of Christ gathers for Eucharist, it makes use of this process to celebrate the paschal mystery as the guiding narrative pattern for the conscience and virtue formation of its members. In chapter 5, "Discerning Out of Mystery," we look more closely at what it means for Christians to live out of the paschal mystery. In this chapter, we offer a concrete way of first discerning out of and then acting according to the mystery of Jesus' passion, death, and resurrection. In our conclusion, we summarize our findings and offer a succinct statement of the role of the Eucharist in the spiritual and moral development of the Christian faithful.

In writing this book, we hope to bring the Church's eucharistic worship to the fore of the present discussion on the relationship between the disciplines of spirituality and moral theology. We see the Eucharist as a point of convergence for these disciplines on many levels: the experiential, the doctrinal, and the scholarly. The Eucharist, we assert, puts us in touch with the mystery of Christ's redeeming love, a mystery that heals and elevates, that not only restores but also transforms. This process of healing and transformation extends to every level of our human makeup and has repercussions, both individually and as a group, for the attitudes we assume, the values we prize, the decisions we make, and the actions we emulate. Through it, our personal and communal narratives flow into Christ's, and his paschal mystery informs every aspect of our existence. As members of his body, we gather at Eucharist to deepen our participation in Christ's suffering, death, and resurrection so that the Easter mystery might permeate every aspect of our lives and lead us further along the path to glory. For this to happen, however, we must first open our hearts and minds to the Lord and humbly recognize our ongoing need for conversion. If we fail in this respect, we will receive little tangible fruit from what we celebrate and the Eucharist itself may well become an empty ritual having little (if any) practical significance for our daily lives.

Dennis J. Billy, CSsR
James Keating

CHAPTER ONE

The Paschal Mystery

We know the importance that Jesus attached to the proclamation of the Kingdom of God in his preaching. It is not just
the creature's recognition of his dependence on his Creator;
it is also the conviction that within history there is at work a
plan, a design, a strategy of harmony and good desired by
God. The Paschal Mystery of the Death and Resurrection of
Jesus has brought this to fulfillment.

Pope John Paul II
General Audience, April 3, 2002

The phrase *paschal mystery* typically refers to the redemptive action of
Christ's passion, death, and resurrection. *The Catechism of the Catholic
Church* tells us that this mystery is at the very heart of the message that
the apostles and believers of every age proclaim to the world. It also
tells us that, through this mystery, God has definitively effected the
world's salvation through the redemptive death of his Son.[1] The biblical roots of the two words comprising the phrase shed important
light on its root meaning. *Paschal* comes from the Greek word
pascha, which itself is derived from the Hebrew term *pesach*, the term
used to designate both the actual event and the annual commemoration of Israel's delivery from slavery in Egypt. The term *mystery*,
from the Greek word *mysterion*, concerns God's plan of salvation for
the world.[2] For Christians, this plan centers on the death and resurrection of Jesus Christ and the historical continuance of this redemptive action in the life and ministry of the church, particularly through
the sacraments. The paschal mystery thus celebrates a new
Passover, when Christ, our paschal lamb, is slain in order to free us
from the slavery of death. This new Passover presupposes a mutual
sharing among the mysteries of God, Christ, and the church. It also
presupposes that "[t]he total and integral figure of the New
Testament Jesus is that of the Jesus of the paschal mystery: incarnate

Son of God, born and become visible *in forma servi*, dead, risen, and now in glory, in a continuous act of communicating to the world the divine life of which He is the perfect and solitary dispenser."[3]

Looking at Human Experience

God's purpose in Christ's paschal mystery is to plumb the depths of human experience in order to heal and elevate it.[4] To understand how Jesus' passion, death, and resurrection achieve this purpose, it is necessary to look at the most common denominators of human experience. This approach may seem strange in an age when human experience is said to be inexorably tied to language and when language itself is a product of a vast interconnecting web of cultural interactions. Christians claim, however, that the Christ event is both transhistorical and transcultural. While rooted in a specific place, time, and cultural milieu, Christ's paschal mystery touches the heart of human experience and speaks to all people, regardless of their moment in history or particular cultural background. Human experience is personal, social, and universal. Each of us has a sense of our own personal identity, of our communal bonds with the various groups to which we belong, and of our ties to all human beings. Our universal bonds with humanity are the constants that define the human situation throughout history. Positively, all human beings share a fundamental dignity by virtue of their being created in the image and likeness of God. Negatively, all are subject to ignorance, weakness of will, faintness of heart, inordinate desire, suffering, and death.[5]

To verify these claims we need only to look at our experience of our own humanity. We struggle to overcome ignorance and petty prejudices. We give in to the allure of passing pleasures, even when we have resolved to avoid them. We isolate ourselves from one another and can easily find ourselves wallowing in doubt and self-pity. We contend against our own envy, greed, and pride—and that of others. Hunger and disease stalk us, either close up or at a distance, while death follows us from the moment we are born. When we examine our experience, we see something lacking within ourselves, but know not what it is. We feel incomplete, yet know not why. We yearn for more out of life, and become disappointed when we do not find it. We yearn for self-transcendence, yet cannot heal the division within our hearts. We long for communion with others, yet cannot find a way to cross the wide chasm that separates us. Our hearts are restless for God, but we know not where or how to find God. When we take the time to reflect upon it, most of us experience a deep, inner ache within our souls. Because we feel threatened by this painful loneliness, most of us have developed sophisticated ways of covering it over, ignoring it, or avoiding it. Few, if any, of us are capable of confronting it head on, mostly because we are afraid of being overwhelmed by it. We are afraid that this deep gnawing pain beneath the surface of our skin reveals to us the true meaning of life. We sense that, when all is said and done, life really has no purpose or meaning. We are haunted by the thought that there may be nothing after death, that we will simply cease to exist, and that we will have lived in vain.

It would be a mistake to give the impression that a person's cultural milieu and place in time have no effect whatsoever on the way these fundamental constants of human experience are perceived and dealt with. To do so would not do justice to the intimate bonds between human experience and culture that have long been demonstrated by the social sciences. Still, the very possibility of a dialogue among cultures presupposes a common language upon which to base an authentic conversation. To be constructive, such a dialogue must focus on those elements of the human universal that both touch the local context and point beyond it. These experiential constants express themselves from one culture to the next by way of likeness and difference. Just as historians, in their study of the past, must posit a certain similarity of time and space in order to reconstruct a historical narrative that can be read and understood by their readers, so too must Christian theologians presuppose an underlying level of universal human experience in all historical epochs and all cultural milieus for the redemptive action of Christ's paschal mystery to unfold. The inculturation of gospel values presupposes this universal dimension of human experience and uses it as the basis for the transformation of local cultures. It recognizes that Christ's paschal mystery touches what is most common in the human condition and promises to transform it. From that promise sprouts the further hope for authentic growth within that culture based on the dignity of the human person, solidarity, and the common good of all humanity.[6]

A Universal Narrative

Christ's paschal mystery heals humanity of its deep inner wound so that it can share in the divine friendship. It does so by doing for humanity what humanity is unable to do for itself. Human experience tells us that, by ourselves alone, we cannot overcome the dark forces within us. Human experience also tells us that, sooner or later, death will snatch us away. The paschal mystery lies at the very heart of the good news, because it proclaims that, in Jesus Christ, God has entered our world and given himself to us completely, to the point of dying for us, in order to become nourishment for us and a source of hope.

From the earliest days of Christianity, this proclamation was made through narrative. The simple affirmation "He is risen!" provides the essential narrative substratum of the Easter mystery. This proclamation asserts that something *happened* to Jesus of Nazareth. What *happened* to him was something that, at one and the same time, was rooted in history and yet far transcended it. Because this proclamation was intended for the great mass of humanity, it was primarily communicated through narrative form. As people pondered what *happened* to Jesus, the narrative of the Easter mystery increasingly grew in size. Projected back in time, Jesus' resurrection presupposed his death and burial. Jesus' death and burial, in turn, presupposed his earlier life and ministry, which presupposed the circumstances surrounding his birth. The circumstances surrounding his birth led to reflections about his divine preexistence. The narrative of the Easter mystery was also projected forward in time. Jesus' resurrection required his eventual return to the Father, and his return to the Father led to the sending of the Spirit. The sending of the Spirit led to the establishment of the church and its mission to preach the gospel to the whole world until Jesus' triumphant return at the end of time.

These narrative projections backward and forward in time enabled the narrative of the Easter mystery to develop along the lines of a gradually expanding circle. Those events closest in time to the resurrection (e.g., Jesus' passion and death; Jesus' ascension and sending of the Spirit) were the earliest additions. Those further away (e.g., his birth and infancy; the growth and spread of the earliest Christian communities) were developed and added later. It must be remembered, however, that the narrative of the Christ event, while rooted in time, also far transcends it. For this reason, we cannot presume a one-to-one correspondence between the developing Easter narrative and the mystery it seeks to express. The relationship between the two is far more elusive. As the New Testament itself attests, numerous narrative constructs are needed to convey an adequate sense of the meaning of the Easter mystery.[7]

Although, strictly speaking, Jesus' paschal mystery concerns only his passion, death, and resurrection, the concept has been extended to all the other elements of the gospel message. As indicated earlier, the paschal mystery "...stands at the center of the Good News that the apostles, and the Church following them, are to proclaim to the world."[8] Because of this central position, the paschal mystery affects every other aspect of the gospel narrative. Take Jesus' death and resurrection out of the picture and the entire narrative movement of the gospel message collapses. Because it stands both in and out of time, moreover, the paschal mystery is able to claim universal significance for humanity. This significance stems from the way Christ and his paschal mystery have become the language through which God addresses the needs of all humanity.[9]

Jesus' paschal mystery offers humanity the promise of redemption. It addresses every lack and existential longing of human experience. Through Jesus' death and resurrection, God announces his decision to take humanity's side in its struggle against death. It manifests God's deep, endearing love for humanity and presents this love as a power the forces of darkness cannot overcome. Begotten by God, Jesus is the New Adam (Rom 5:12–19), the firstborn of a new humanity (Rom 8:29). He is the high priest of the new and eternal covenant between God and his people (Heb 4:14). Through Jesus, humanity has become divinized. This process of divinization extends to the human universal and is concretized in each individual through a divine adoption. Through Jesus, each human being has the opportunity of becoming an adopted son or daughter of God and, because of this adoption, can overcome the weakness of the human condition. Ignorance, weakness of will, faintness of heart, inordinate desire, suffering, and death no longer have a stranglehold over us. Their time has passed. Humanity's narrative is now intrinsically tied to the narrative of Christ. The paschal mystery now stands at the center of our lives. We cut ourselves off from it only by freely refusing to accept it.[10]

Models of Redemption[11]

Christ's paschal mystery is the defining moment of human history. It changed, is changing, and will change the course of that history and its final outcome. The initial experience of the Risen Christ manifested itself in narrative form and eventually through set doctrinal formulas. A fundamental continuity exists in this movement from experience to narrative to doctrine. We profess the creed because of the gospel narratives upon which it is based and the experiences of the Risen Lord by the apostles and early followers of Jesus that gave rise to them. Catholic teaching presupposes this continuity between experience, narrative, and doctrine, and the relationship is mutually beneficial. Doctrine protects narrative and experience from dangerous heterodox tendencies; experience and narrative, in turn, provide doctrine with a rich existential substratum from which to draw. Nowhere is this more true than in the church's teaching on the redemption, of which there have been four significant formulations in the history of Christian thought: ransom, satisfaction, subjective atonement, and liberation.

Considered the classical expression of the patristic and early medieval periods, redemption as *ransom* regards humanity as an insignificant onlooker in a cosmic battle between God and the celestial host, on the one hand, and Lucifer and the powers of the underworld, on the other. Couched in mythic language, it considers Christ's incarnation, passion, and death as the ransom that had to be paid for humanity's release from the terrible snare of death, the latter seen as a privilege won by Satan on account of Adam's sin.

First developed by Anselm of Canterbury in the *Cur Deus homo* (ca. 1098), redemption as *satisfaction* understands Christ's suffering and death as the voluntary manifestation of divine mercy needed to meet the requirements of the divine justice directed against humanity on account of Adam's infinite transgression. Rooted in the legal structures and language of feudal vassalage, it guides redemption theory away from a cosmic confrontation between God and the devil and concentrates, instead, on the broken relationship between a just and loving God, on the one hand, and a sinful human race, on the other. In this presentation of redemption theory, the devil fades to the background, while God and humanity relate to each other more directly, that is, through a divine/human mediator.

The subjective atonement (or moral) theory rejected both the ransom and satisfaction models. First developed by the scholastic theologian Peter Abelard and adopted centuries later by a number of the proponents of Protestant Liberalism, it insists that Jesus died on the cross not to ransom us from Satan or to satisfy God's justice, but to give us an example, that is, to show us how to love. It uses a variety of poetic images to convey the idea that Jesus' death on the cross reveals to those who experience it the true meaning of love. Jesus' humble act of total self-surrendering love is meant to move us and evoke from us a similar response. This approach to redemption relativized the concept of sin and emphasized humanity's capacity—both individually and socially—to lead the moral life.

In the twentieth century, the exploitive effects of the ideologies of power—fascism, Marxism, and capitalism—and their large-scale exploitation of humanity eventually led theologians to develop yet another theory, that is, redemption as *liberation*. Rooted in an eschatology of actively working for the realization of the kingdom in the present, this approach locates evil in corrupt societal structures designed to oppress the poor for the advantage of a privileged elite. Redemption, here, has to do with the realization of human solidarity through the universal call to justice.

This is not the place to go into the finer points of the above models. The relationship of the ransom model to Mark 10:45 and Matthew 20:28, Aquinas's elaboration of Anselm's satisfaction theory, Luther's reaction against the heavily legal emphasis of satisfaction and his subsequent return to the ransom approach, Catholicism's deep suspicion of subjective atonement and its cautious magisterial response to the theologies of liberation have all been documented elsewhere and need not be repeated.[12] What does need to be developed, however, is precisely what has been missing in nearly all recent discussions of redemption theory, that is, the specific contribution of each of these models to the church's actual understanding of the mystery of redemption.

These contributions become clear when the theories themselves are looked at in the light of the specific relationship(s) each addresses. The ransom model, for example, uses mythic language within a predominantly Neoplatonic framework to express the cosmic relationship between the forces of good and evil. The satisfaction model, in turn, employs legal language and the Anselmian notion of necessary reasons in order to express the importance of humanity's relationship to the divine. The subjective model adopts the rational optimism of the Enlightenment to reveal the internal processes of the moral life. The liberation model embraces the concepts of contemporary political analysis to emphasize the need for just social structures. Each theory focuses on a different type of relationship: ransom on "the cosmic," satisfaction on "the divine and human," the subjective on "the inner personal," and liberation on "the societal." In their respective positions, these relations describe the realities of divine-human unrelation, divine-human relation, human self-relation, and human social relation. Each makes a specific contribution to our understanding of redemption theory.

To speak of redemption in terms of *divine-human unrelation* is to move the concerns of humanity from the center to the periphery of God's providential plan. Here, humanity sees itself not as the center of God's undivided attention, but in strong creaturely solidarity with the entire universe. In doing so, it recognizes that the scope of the redemption includes elements far beyond its own comprehension and extends far beyond its own need for salvific grace. Here, humanity understands that the struggle against evil is not a mere anthropocentric concern and cannot focus solely on its own potential for sin.

To speak of redemption in terms of *divine-human relation* is to look at the way humanity actually does become the center of God's salvific plan. Created in God's image and called to walk with God in paradise, humanity recognizes the extent to which sin has disrupted its relationship with God and understands that its hope rests only in the saving love of Christ. Here, the soteriological principle that "God became human so that humanity might become divine"[13] is of fundamental significance: humanity's divinization is contingent on God's humanization; in this all-embracing redemptive moment, God meets man and woman through the mediation of his Son, the God-Man.

To speak of redemption in terms of *human self-relation* is to emphasize the effects of this process of divinization on the person and to call attention to the way in which each individual shares in God's providential plan. Cooperation with this plan becomes the sign of whether or not a person can actually be considered the master of his or her own actions. Here, redemption manifests itself as an inner conversion toward the standards of a just and moral life. Grace is experienced in a highly personal, subjective manner; it moves the person to lead a virtuous life out of sheer love for God.

To speak of redemption in terms of *human social relation* is to recognize the social character of human existence and to believe in the potential of a divinely inspired humanity to transform not only individuals, but even the political and economic structures by which they live. Here, redemption takes place within the parameters of humanity's ongoing earthly existence rather than through the promise of an "otherworldly" reward or in the eschatological reality of some past or future age. Redemption occurs in humanity's liberation of the oppressed by means of its continuing search for social justice.

These relations are to be thought of as complementary movements of the one redemptive mystery. When taken as such, they demonstrate the limited capacity of any language (be it mythic, juridic, subjective, social) or any philosophy (be it Neoplatonic, scholastic, Cartesian, or Marxist) or any historical epoch (be it the patristic, medieval, Enlightened, or postmodern) to capture fully the mystery it seeks to express. While they obviously fall short of providing a complete description of the redemptive mystery as a whole, it would be fair to say that each theory succeeds in highlighting at least one of the doctrine's essential salvific relations. In this respect, the mystery of the redemption can be thought of as containing facets of the cosmic, the divine and human, the subjective, and the social. To deny any one of these important components would impoverish the significance of the mystery and be unfaithful to the doctrine's theological tradition.[14]

When seen in this light, the work of redemption concerns the manifestation of the divine in the person of Christ under four interrelated aspects: (1) divine-human unrelation, through which humanity finds its place in the universal macrocosm of its divine Creator, (2) divine-human relation, through which humanity recognizes in the suffering of Christ the salvific love of a personal God, (3) human self-relation, through which a person's experience of that love manifests itself in inner conversion to a life of virtue, and (4) human social relation, through which humanity struggles to realize the presence of the kingdom within the historical structures of its present earthly existence. Each of these aspects reveals an essential feature of the Christ event, the particular significance of which is variously interpreted according to the changing needs and theological comprehension of the times.

The operative interpretive principle in this description rests on the assumption that, while the mystery of the redemption remains constant for all time and is always inclusive of the four relational components outlined above, particular theological formulations will vary according to the predominant linguistic, philosophical, and cultural needs of the historical epoch in question. Any particular period will tend to emphasize one relational component, sometimes to the exclusion of the others: the patristic period emphasized the cosmic element; the high middle ages, that of the human-divine encounter; the Enlightenment, the subjective; the postmodern, that of political and societal liberation. The above approach is sufficiently malleable to adapt to changing theological and philosophical perceptions while, at the same time, acquitting itself of the charges of historical relativism. It does so by giving proportional emphasis to both the kataphatic and apophatic aspects of theological language and by employing a complementary approach to the various historical attempts at giving the mystery of the redemption some kind of doctrinal formulation.

A Necessary Corrective

These various theories developed to explain the mystery of redemption bring out some of the inherent limitations of human language. Whatever its strengths, no one theory is capable of exhausting the depths of the mystery it tries to express. The paschal mystery is closely allied to the mystery of redemption and, in many respects, depends on it as a raison d'être. The mystery of redemption must be viewed in the light of God's threefold economic plan of creation, redemption, and sanctification. While all the persons of the Trinity are intimately involved in every aspect of this threefold work, primary roles are often assigned to God the Father for the work of Creation, God the Son for the work of redemption, and God the Holy Spirit for the work of sanctification.[15]

When seen in this light, the mystery of redemption is a part of a narrative that flows from the very heart of the Triune God. In Christianity, the mystery of God is rooted in the mystery of love. This mystery is considered to be identical with the good, a term that classical philosophical thought has taken to be "self-diffusive."[16] Once assimilated into Christian theology, this notion presents God as a personal Triune mystery whose very nature seeks to pour itself out freely in loving acts of creation, redemption, and sanctification. In this respect, the narrative of the paschal mystery is a part of a larger metanarrative that flows from the heart of the divine mystery and ultimately returns to it. To be more specific, the paschal mystery of Christ's passion, death, and resurrection is the practical means by which God implements his providential plan for humanity's redemption. Down through the ages, theologians have debated whether Christ's passion, death, and resurrection were the only way to implement such a plan. Most have concluded that, if it was not the only possible plan, it was by far the most fitting and most revelatory of the mystery of God's love for humanity.[17] In any case, the paschal mystery is subject to the same limitations of human expression as the mysteries associated with the metanarrative of the divine economy, most especially with the mystery of redemption. When seen in this light, it is important to note that the various elements of the paschal mystery (e.g., Jesus' passion, his death, his resurrection) have been interpreted in various ways regarding their roles in the mystery of redemption.

In the past, Jesus' death on the cross was placed at the center of redemptive theory, while his prior suffering and his resurrection and ascension were viewed as secondary features and, in some instances, purely accidental.[18] This imbalance in thought needs to be corrected if the paschal mystery is to be truly understood as lying at the very heart of the gospel proclamation. Rather than focusing on a single aspect of the mystery (e.g., the cross or the resurrection), it would be much more beneficial to view the mystery itself in its entirety and to use it as a fundamental point of departure for speaking about the healing and elevating effects of humanity's redemption. In this respect, it would be wise to consider the paschal mystery in its wider context, the one that focuses on the entire gambit of Christ's entrance and departure from our world, rather than simply on his passion, death, and resurrection.[19]

The rationale for this wider approach comes from the aforementioned soteriological principle first formulated by St. Athanasius of Alexandria, "God became human so that humanity might become divine."[20] This principle has two important strengths. First, it views humanity's redemption specifically in the context of its divinization, a process that emphasizes the close bonds between redemption and the process of sanctification. Second, it shifts the focus of redemption away from Jesus' cross and resurrection to the mystery of his incarnation. In doing so, it challenges us to reconsider our presuppositions about the nature of Christ's paschal mystery and encourages us to think of it in terms of a much wider redemptive narrative. When seen in this light, Jesus' passion, death, and resurrection will continue to remain at the center of the gospel proclamation. That center, however, cannot be presented as a center apart from the various other elements that bring it into focus. The divine self-emptying (i.e., *kenosis*) described by Paul in his letter to the Philippians (Phil 2:6–11) occurs not just during the death and resurrection of Jesus, but in the mystery of God becoming human, a movement that can be understood only as a visible expression (a sacrament, if you will) of the eternal self-emptying existing in the very heart of the Godhead itself. When seen in this light, the paschal mystery concerns the life-giving love lying at the heart of the divine self-emptying. As such, it too lies in the heart of God himself: "There is a cross in God before the wood is seen on Calvary."[21]

A Revelatory Function

When we speak of the paschal mystery in this fuller sense and locate it within the very heart of the Triune God, its important revelatory dimensions stand out. Jesus of Nazareth represents the fullness of God's revelation to humanity. His entire life represents a loving relationship with *Abba,* his Father in heaven. His paschal mystery demonstrates his full obedience to his Father's plan for humanity. His obedience to the Father unto death is a manifestation of his love for the Father. His resurrection by the Father is a manifestation of the Father's love for him, and by virtue of the incarnation, for all humanity. When seen in this light, Christ's paschal mystery is tied not only to the economic plan of the Trinity (specifically, the redemption), but also to the intimate relations within the Trinity itself (i.e., the love between Father and Son).

To speak of the paschal mystery as a revelation of the Son's love for the Father and the Father's love for the Son is another way of speaking about the revelation of the Spirit. The Holy Spirit is the bond of love existing between the Father and Son. It was this love that was made manifest in Christ's paschal mystery; it was this love that the disciples experienced at Pentecost and that moves the body of Christ, the church, in its proclamation of the good news. This love validates the transhistorical and transcendental dimensions of the paschal mystery. By virtue of its connection with God's economic plan of redemption, the paschal mystery extends to all of human history, both before and after the Christ event. By virtue of its revelatory function, the paschal mystery has transcendent significance in that it manifests the fullness of love within the very heart of God. Both dimensions of the paschal mystery are important if we wish to understand its ongoing significance for us. We are historical beings who live in a particular moment in space and time. As a species, however, our existence has already crossed millions of years and may well extend into the future for centuries to come. Our destiny as both individuals and as a species, however, is to rest in the heart of the divine mystery. We have come from the mind of God, and our destiny is to return there. The paschal mystery reminds us of our origins, our earthly lives, and our eternal destiny.[22]

Another way of looking at the revelatory function of the paschal mystery is to look at the various levels of meaning within it. The paschal mystery resides: (1) in the mystery of the Triune God, (2) in the mystery of Christ, the Word-made-flesh, and (3) in the mystery of the body of Christ, the church.[23] These levels are ordered hierarchically. The presence of the paschal mystery in the church presupposes its presence in the mystery of Christ that, in turn, presupposes its presence in the heart of the Trinity. This hierarchical ordering within the paschal mystery creates a continuum of participation from God through Christ to humanity. Through the paschal mystery, the innermost heart of God is revealed to the heart of the Son and, through him, to the heart of humanity. Through the paschal mystery, Christ has become the sacrament of God; the church, in turn, is established as the sacrament of Christ.[24] The sacraments of the church immerse us in the paschal mystery of Christ only because of this hierarchical ordering that leads the faithful through Christ to a real participation in the inner life of the Trinity. We should never forget that the word *sacrament* comes from the Latin word *sacramentum*, which is a rendering of the Greek word for *mysterion*, meaning *mystery*.[25] When seen in this light, the paschal mystery can be thought of as a *sacramentum* that has its origins in the inner life of the Trinity, communicates the life of the Trinity, and reveals its inner nature. A sacrament, as such, both communicates grace and reveals something hidden. For Christians, all sacraments flow from the mystery of the Triune God. This mystery rests at the summit of the Catholic hierarchy of truths and at the heart of the gospel (or, for that matter, any) narrative: "The Blessed Trinity and Undivided Unity of God is the beginning, the middle, and the end of all our storytelling."[26]

The revelatory character of the paschal mystery also helps us to see the narrative that issues from it in a different light. We have already seen how the center of that narrative lies in the proclamation of the death and resurrection of Christ and how it builds out in an expanding circle to embrace not only Jesus' entire life on this earth, but also his preexistence in the Trinity and his transformed life after death. We have also seen how the paschal mystery is also a part of a much wider metanarrative that embraces the economic plan of the Trinity and its origins in the inner relations of love among the Father, Son, and Holy Spirit. The universal narrative of the paschal mystery reveals God's love to us and releases the power of God's saving grace. It touches our human condition and leads us to God. It can do so, however, only because it reveals to us something of what God is and raises within us the hope that our inner yearning for union with the divine will one day be met.

Rooted in God, Jesus Christ, and the church, the paschal mystery uses word and sacrament to immerse us in God's providential plan of redemption. The purpose of this plan is to heal humanity of its wounds and to transform it so that it might share in the intimate life of the Trinity. Another name for our sharing in this intimate life is *divinization*. Because of Jesus' paschal mystery, we who share in Jesus' humanity also participate in his divine sonship. As adopted sons and daughters of the Father, we join in God's redemptive plan for humanity and become active participants in the living narrative of Christ's paschal mystery in our own historical moment. What has happened to Christ also happens to the members of his body, the church. In this way, the paschal mystery becomes relevant to us, here and now, as a narrative of healing and transformation that reveals to us the fullness of our own inner nature and the fullness of life promised by Christ to his disciples.

Adopted Sons and Daughters

Christ's paschal mystery reveals the depths of God's love for us and enables us to share in it intimately. This gift is bestowed on us from above. It is not something we have a right to or can simply bargain for. It comes to us through a divine initiative, that is, God's decision to enter his Creation and to draw it to himself in such a way that it partakes of his own inner life. Through the paschal mystery, God enters human experience and reveals the extent of his love for us. He does so in order that we might be able to enter into the divine experience and reveal the extent of our love for him. We can do so, however, only within the bounds of our creaturely limitations. The process of divinization initiated through the paschal mystery makes us *God-like*. It does not, however, take away our creaturely identity by absorbing us into the divine nature. Christ enters our world to join humanity's experience to the experience of the divine. For this to happen, however, humanity's experience must be elevated and thoroughly transformed. This glorious change takes place in Christ's passion, death, and resurrection. Through it, humanity is made anew so that it can enter into the presence of the Father. This remaking involves a healing of our inner wounds so that we are capable of being God-centered rather than self-centered. The process begins at baptism, when Christ immerses us in his paschal mystery and makes us a part of the new humanity. As a result of this action, the Father looks upon us as he looks upon his only begotten Son. He treats us as if we were his own sons and daughters. With Jesus, we are able to turn to the Father and cry out to him, "Abba, Father" (Rom 8:15).

Christ's paschal mystery establishes an intimate, loving bond between God and humanity. The whole purpose of the paschal mystery is to make things right between God and humanity. Human experience tells us that this bond existed once before, but was somehow broken; we sense, moreover, that it was somehow our own doing. Christ's paschal mystery enables humanity to overcome its primordial estrangement from God. It puts things right between us and, as is often the case with repaired relationships, helps us to enjoy an even deeper intimacy. We do not understand exactly how things are put right with God through the paschal mystery. Through the eyes of faith, all we can say is that God refused to abandon us, but took the initiative to heal the relationship and to make it even stronger. The difference in the relationship is Christ. He is now the eternal mediator between the human and divine. He mediates this bond by virtue of his becoming man and by virtue of his passion, death, and resurrection. Because we approach the Father only through, with, and in Christ, our relationship to the Father is not direct, but participative. We are children of the Father, by virtue of our share in Christ's divine sonship. Through Christ, the Father has adopted us as his own. Through Christ, we share in the love of the Father. Through Christ, we are able to return the Father's love and live our lives according to the ways of the Spirit.

By making us adopted sons and daughters of the Father, Christ's paschal mystery opens up for us the life of the Spirit. Through Christ, we are able to share in the intimate bond of love that unites the Father and his only begotten Son. That bond is the person of the Holy Spirit. Our sharing in this bond manifests itself in the Spirit's dwelling within our hearts, which is one of the primary results of Christ's paschal mystery. The reestablishment of the relationship between God and humanity manifests itself concretely in our lives through the gift of the Spirit. This gift is the sign of our participated, adoptive sonship, reminding us of who we are and what we are destined to become. God is able to dwell within our hearts because, through Christ, we are able to dwell in the heart of God. The paschal mystery makes this possible. Christ's redemptive action prepares the way for the coming of the Spirit and its sanctifying role in the lives of the faithful. Pentecost marks the beginning of a new phase in God's economic plan. Just as God's creative plan precedes and makes possible his redemptive plan, so now must his redemptive plan precede and make possible his plan of sanctification.

Friendship with Christ

An integral part of our search for holiness involves putting on the mind of Christ. Our new relationship with the Father is preceded by the newly forged friendship we have with Christ and with one another. Christ is not only our Lord and master, but also a friend and brother to us. Our friendship with Christ involves benevolence, reciprocity, and a mutual indwelling. He actively seeks our well-being as we try to do the same. The result is an experience of mutual self-discovery. We find ourselves in Christ, while Christ lives out his life in us and discovers himself anew.[27] Friends influence one another for the good. Our friendship with Christ gradually shapes us into a likeness of himself as we strive to be like him in all things. We strive to think like him, feel like him, talk like him, and act like him. We seek to adopt the same values and the same attitudes. We clothe ourselves in his teachings and way of life confident that, in time, his compassion and love will bring about a change in us. Christ, for his part, receives from us the opportunity to extend his reign of love through space and time. Through us, he once again lives the drama of his paschal mystery for the salvation of the world. Our lives are closely bound up with his, as are our deaths—and our eternal destiny. With the apostle Paul, each of us can say: "…it is no longer I who live, but it is Christ who lives in me" (Gal 2:20). We can say this because, through his paschal mystery, Christ has put to death the old self and given rise to the new. Christ, the New Adam, invites us to be a part of the new Creation. Through him, we are made anew by the power of his Spirit.

Because of our friendship with Christ, we find new meaning in the call to discipleship. Jesus said, "No one has greater love than this, to lay down one's life for one's friends" (John 15:13). Jesus laid down his life for us; we, in turn, lay down our lives for others through a life of dedicated ministry and service. In doing so, we allow Christ to live out his paschal mystery anew: we become sharers in his passion, death, and resurrection; we also participate in the mystery of Christ's redemptive action. By drawing us into the peace of his friendship, Christ makes us members of his body. In the world today, he lives, suffers, dies, and rises, in and through the members of his body. When seen in this light, the life and death drama of Christ's paschal mystery continues in the life and mission of the church. Like Christ, the church is human and divine. Like Christ, the church lives in solidarity with the poor and the oppressed, preaching a message of liberation from sin and death. Like Christ, the church reaches out to those who are neglected and in need. Like Christ, the church is the sacramental presence of the Father's love in space and time. Christ is present in his church and acts through it. He does so primarily through its liturgical worship, which, especially through the sacraments of baptism and the Eucharist, makes the paschal mystery really present to those participating.

The sacraments of the church are actions of Christ; through them, Christ continues to live out his paschal mystery. For this reason, they are enduring signs of Christ's love for us. When the church celebrates the sacraments, the power of Christ's paschal mystery manifests itself to the eyes of faith, and only those with faith can see the mystery taking shape. This mystery gives rise to hope within the hearts of the faithful and encourages them all the more to embrace the love of God in their lives. The sacraments of the church are concrete and visible signs of God's love for the world. Christ acts through them to touch us, to impart his life to us, to send us his Spirit, to nourish us, to strengthen us, to call us, and to anoint us. The sacraments are visible mysteries that not only speak of God's love, but also make it present. They are palpable signs of Christ's friendship, inviting us to enter more and more deeply into the mystery of his love. Through the sacraments, Christ's paschal mystery becomes present to us in very concrete, tangible ways. The sacraments make Christ's paschal mystery real for us by giving us access to his redeeming love.

Observations

The above presentation of the centrality of Christ's paschal mystery to the Christian faith lends itself to a number of observations concerning its relevance to the spiritual moral life. While it will not be possible to exhaust the spiritual and moral implications of Christ's passion, death, and resurrection, some of the more significant points can be identified and commented upon. Ten in particular come to mind.

1. As presented above, the paschal mystery, while centered in the passion, death, and resurrection of Christ, has a wider meaning extending to the incarnation and to Jesus' life and ministry. It also forms part of the larger narrative pertaining to God's providential plan of creation, redemption, and sanctification. We have also seen that it pertains not only to God's economic plan, but also to the internal relations within the Trinity itself. The reason for this wider context stems from the broad scope of God's providential plan for humanity. To be understood properly, Christ's paschal mystery must be seen as an integral part of that providential plan, one that finds its source not only in God's external relations with his creation, but also in God's own immanent self-relations. A continuity necessarily exists between these internal self-relations and the divine economic activity. The nature of this continuity lies in the free and self-diffusive nature of God's love. The mysteries of creation,

redemption, and humanity's sanctification flow from the mystery of the divine love. Christ's paschal mystery flows from this love in the same way and necessarily has its roots in the heart of the Trinity. At the same time, it also has its roots in the human heart of Christ. The continuity between being and action in God has certain implications for the nature of the Christian spiritual moral life. Our actions, for example, must flow from our internal convictions and be centered in a sincere desire to be a part of God's providential plan for the world. They must also be rooted in the human heart of Christ and its determined desire to carry out the will of the Father.

2. At its root, Christ's paschal mystery represents the power of love to overcome the power of death. The human heart finds both powers vying for its allegiance and, at times, the situation of the world is such that it seems as though the powers of death have the upper hand. The power of death has its origins in evil, a mystery that classical Christian theology claims has its roots in a revolt against God by angelic powers and in humanity's free and willful decision to cut itself off from fellowship with God. The defeat of death signals humanity's triumph through Christ over the very forces that deprive it of its dignity and destiny in the heart of the divine. Attempts to extract the Christian doctrine of original sin from a literal interpretation of the account of the fall of man in the book of Genesis (3) have identified certain key affirmations that must not be compromised. Expressed in various ways over the course of time, the Christian doctrine of the fall teaches five fundamental truths: the fundamental goodness of creation, humanity's creation in the image and likeness of God, the need for humanity's redemption (i.e., healing and divinization), the weakness of creaturely limitation, and the need for Christ's grace in baptism. In its confrontation with death, Christ's paschal mystery affirms each of these essential truths of humanity's creation, redemption, and sanctification. It does so by means of a divine embrace of death that destroys death for the sake of humanity's radical transformation. This transformation takes place through a process of healing and elevation that allows humanity to experience intimacy with the divine more deeply than ever before. This intimacy with the divine moves Christians to fight against evil and the forces of death by embracing a "culture of life."[28] By embracing life in all its dimensions, from conception to the grave, Christians

proclaim the truth of Christ's paschal mystery and mediate its presence to the world through their thoughts, words, and deeds.

3. The eschatological, "already-but-not-yet" dimension of Christ's paschal mystery invites Christians to take an active role in bringing about the coming of the kingdom. Christ may have risen from the dead, but human experience tells us that death still holds powerful sway over human lives. The defeat of death has already taken place, but is also still to come. The coming of the kingdom depends, at least in part, on how the forces of death are dealt with in the present. Christ's paschal mystery lives on in the life of his body, the church. As members of his body, we are called not only to proclaim Christ's paschal mystery, but to embrace it with our lives. Doing so helps us to view death in an entirely different way. Because of our communion with Christ, we recognize that death ultimately has no power over us. We are able to stare it in the eyes and look beyond it. Jesus' defeat of death kindles in us the hope that we too shall rise. We live in this hope and allow it to shape our actions. Everything in our lives is oriented toward this future triumph over death. At the Eucharist, we proclaim with believers throughout the world: "Christ has died. Christ has risen. Christ will come again." Christ's future coming, we believe, will usher in the final defeat of death. As we await his coming, our actions in the world take on a decidedly eschatological dimension. We struggle against the "culture of death"[29] not because we believe that we can defeat it through our own efforts and by our own accord, but because we believe that what was initiated on Easter morning will come to term at the consummation and end of time. Our business, in the meantime, is to proclaim the good news and to embrace it with lives dedicated to the affirmation of life and its ongoing transformation in all respects.

4. The paschal mystery permeates our life and ministry just as it did the life and ministry of Jesus of Nazareth. Through our immersion into his death and resurrection at baptism, we become sharers in Jesus' redemptive action. This action culminates in his passion, death, and resurrection, but is already present in Jesus' hidden and public life. The paschal mystery defines Jesus' life on earth. Through it, he discovers the Father's will and carries it out in an action of heroic self-offering. Jesus' entire life was a preparation for this action. His life and public ministry pointed to it and were validated by it. Jesus' life and ministry provide the spiritual and moral context

through which the drama of his passion, death, and resurrection plays itself out. The paschal mystery, in other words, did not take place in a historical vacuum: it did not do so in Jesus' day; it does not do so in our own. Our closeness to Christ allows for a deep participation in his paschal mystery. Because of its transhistorical dimension, Christ's paschal mystery extends into time and space through the members of his living body. Through baptism, we become members of that living body. Everything in our lives is a preparation for the role we play in it. We live with Christ, so that we might die and rise with him; our actions derive their meaning and value from Christ's paschal mystery. The narrative of our lives is thus closely bound up with Christ: he has entered our human story so that we might enter his. The measure of our actions is the degree to which they lead us to an even deeper participation in his redemptive action.

5. Christ's paschal mystery manifests itself fully in the celebration of the liturgy, especially during the Eucharist. The liturgy is the source and summit of the church's life. When celebrating the sacraments, the church celebrates Christ's paschal mystery and becomes more deeply incorporated into it. These actions of Christ have an effect on the church and all its members. They open for us the channels of grace that allow us to move in close concert with the promptings of the Spirit. Through the liturgy, we worship God the Father, through Christ and in the Spirit. Life in the Spirit is not possible apart from the actions of Christ manifested in the church's liturgical celebrations. Everything in the Christian life is oriented toward them; everything flows from them. The spiritual moral life of the Christian is intimately bound up with the church's worship: *lex orandi, lex credendi, lex agendi.*[30] The church's prayer influences what it believes and how it acts. The church's sacraments are visible signs of Christ's presence with his people. They remind us that his passion, death, and resurrection are still a vital force in the world. When we participate in the liturgy, we affirm our belief in Christ and recommit ourselves to act in the world as members of his body. We come in contact with Christ's paschal mystery first and foremost through our participation in the liturgy. The communion we share with Christ and with one another as a result of the church's liturgical celebration moves us to live out our vocations in a spirit of generosity and service. It also moves us to work on behalf of the poor and oppressed for

the cause of social justice. The liturgy conforms us to Christ and, in doing so, seeks to shape our spiritual and moral lives. Our active participation in the liturgy allows God to work in our lives in ways even beyond our conscious awareness.

6. By immersing us in his paschal mystery, Christ reveals to us the true meaning of discipleship. Jesus said, "If any want to become my followers, let them deny themselves and take up their cross and follow me" (Mark 8:34). Discipleship touches the heart of an individual. It requires a basic change in a person's outlook on life. To follow in Christ's footsteps, we are called to *metanoia*, a fundamental conversion in our lives that moves us out of ourselves and a life of self-centeredness to instead lead lives that are totally dedicated to the service of God and others. Christ's paschal mystery reminds us that we are completely unable to bring this change about through our own efforts. Jesus' passion, death, and resurrection alone can effect a change in the depths of our humanity that, when applied to us individually, enables us to live as he lived. Jesus' passion and death remind us of the suffering we are called to undergo for the sake of the kingdom. His resurrection and ascension remind us that we are to live in hope of the complete transformation of our lives and a life of future glory. Christ's paschal mystery is more than a mere reminder of how we should conduct ourselves as his disciples; it incorporates us into the mystery of Christ's redemptive love and, in doing so, enables us to live and die and rise in, through, and with Christ. Because of the paschal mystery Jesus calls us his friends, not servants or slaves (cf. John 15:15). The true disciple is a friend of Christ, someone who dwells in Christ's heart and who allows Christ to reciprocate. The paschal mystery shapes our spiritual moral lives by allowing us to enjoy the friendship of Christ. To be a saint is to be called a "friend of God."[31] Christ's paschal mystery allows these bonds of friendship to take shape and to flourish. We, in turn, are called to do the same for those we serve.

7. Although Christ's paschal mystery touches every dimension of human existence, its major work lies in the changes it brings about in humanity as a whole. Over the course of time, this universal aspect of the paschal mystery has been presented in various ways. Saint Paul talked of Christ being the New Adam, the firstborn of a new humanity who would overcome the power of sin and death (Rom 5:12–14). In his doctrine of redemption, Saint Augustine used

the concept of "seminal nature"[32] to explain how Christ's paschal mystery could overturn the disastrous results that a single sin would wreak upon humanity. In the post–Vatican II era, theologians have found other ways of expressing humanity's universal experience of sin and how the passion, death, and resurrection of Jesus seek to address it.[33] However it may be expressed, the paschal mystery must be presented in terms of Christ's triumph over death and the implications this has for all of humanity. Death is common to all human beings. Christ's paschal mystery represents a decisive defeat of death, which ultimately must loosen its hold on humanity and release it. Justice is not done to Christ's paschal mystery when its universal claims for humanity are neglected or watered down. The redemptive action of Christ embraces humanity not simply in the present moment, but across the whole of history. Its purpose is to reestablish humanity on a more secure footing, one where death will no longer reign over it and where sin will no longer be able to set down its roots in the human heart.

8. In addition to touching humanity at its most basic, universal level, Christ's paschal mystery also addresses the social dimension of its experience. During his life on earth, Christ gathered around him a community of followers. At Pentecost, that group received the Holy Spirit, who forged among them deep bonds of communion. This community of believers exists by virtue of Christ's paschal mystery. Through his passion, death, and resurrection, Christ revealed to us the fullness of God's love for the world. For believers, that love is today experienced and lived out first and foremost through the community of believers. This is so because God's love, as the paschal mystery has revealed to us, is primarily communitarian in nature. Christ accepted death on the cross out of his love for the Father's will. That love is the bond of the Spirit, which the Risen Christ released upon the church at Pentecost. Because of the presence of the Spirit, the community of believers is called to forge bonds of community among each other and with the world, which it does by means of proclamation and dialogue. By proclaiming Christ's paschal mystery and by entering into bonds of communion with those who have yet to believe in the reality of the Risen Lord, Christians become instruments of God's love in the world today. The practice of this "spirituality of communion"[34] cannot be done through human efforts alone. We are able to live in communion with others,

only because we are able to live in communion with God. We live in communion with God, however, only by virtue of Christ's paschal mystery. Life in communion is a primary goal of redeemed humanity's social agenda. It is made possible by the movement of the Spirit, who has been poured out on the community of believers as a result of Christ's passion, death, and resurrection.

9. Christ's paschal mystery also touches us as individuals. It promises to transform every aspect of our personal makeup: the physical, intellectual, emotional, spiritual, and the social. When we are incorporated into Christ's passion, death, and resurrection at baptism, we become adopted sons and daughters of God. Made possible by Christ, this new relationship with God initiates a process of spiritual and moral conversion that culminates in our total divinization in the heart of God's love. Christ's paschal mystery thus has repercussions not only for humanity's universal and communal levels, but also for the personal. His death and resurrection make it possible for each of us to enjoy a close, intimate relationship with God. "Paradise for God...is the human heart," the saying goes.[35] This phrase reveals God's intense yearning both to love and to receive the love of each and every human person. If it is to have any meaning at all, Christ's passion, death, and resurrection must ultimately touch us, as individuals, in the very core of our being. Once it does, it gradually redounds to every other dimension of our personal anthropological makeup. This transforming effect takes place through the power of the Spirit unleashed by the Risen Christ to dwell within our hearts. The indwelling of the Holy Spirit is thus a sign of Christ's paschal mystery at work within our lives. Its gifts and fruits point to the peace of Christ's reign already present in our midst and in our hearts. The more we are open to the Spirit's movement in our lives, the more intimate will our relationship be to Christ and to the Father. Christ's paschal mystery promises us that the time will come when the Spirit's presence will be so prevalent in our lives that the power of the Risen Christ will transform us completely and carry us into the heart of God's love. The goal of Christ's paschal mystery is to make possible an intimate divine and human communion. Because of it, God dwells in us, and we in God. Everything else is secondary.

10. Finally, Christ's paschal mystery affects not only humanity, but also God himself by changing forever the way God relates to humanity. Through Christ's passion and death, God has bound him-

self to our human situation. If in the incarnation God has entered our world and become one of us, then by Christ's passion and death he has embraced human experience to the fullest, making it a part of his own destiny. It is only because God has entered the depths of human experience that he is able to transform it from the inside out. Doing so, however, also brings about a change in God. Such a claim may sound strange to Christians who are used to speaking of God's impassibility and immutability. The Christian doctrine of God, however, claims, first and foremost, that God is mystery. What better way to preserve a sense of this mystery than by juxtaposing contrary claims about God's nature? Such a coincidence of opposites has, in fact, taken place for some time in Christianity's fusion of the Greek and Hebrew understandings of God. While the former focused on God's detached and changeless perfection, the latter emphasized God's personal characteristics and his propensity for intervening in human history. Christ's paschal mystery brings this process one step further. Through it, humanity and divinity are now thrust together in close proximity. Jesus Christ, the Incarnate Son of God, embraces death, overcomes it, and now sits at the right hand of the Father. Through him, we have become adopted sons and daughters of God; we too enjoy a privileged place in the kingdom of God. This special dignity, however, carries with it great responsibilities. As God's sons and daughters, our lives must reflect that dignity and help others to recognize it in themselves.

Concluding Remarks

Because the paschal mystery lies at the very heart of the gospel message, it must be proclaimed with conviction. If it is not, then something is seriously wrong with our understanding of it. It cannot be the very heart of the gospel message if it does not move and propel us to change. To proclaim the paschal mystery with conviction, however, we must look at it in a way that makes it comprehensible to our present-day sensibilities. Such a task can be daunting, to say the least. No mystery will ever make sense to us fully. By its very nature, it must remain elusive (even incomprehensible) if it is to evoke from us the awe and wonder it deserves.

This chapter has looked at Christ's paschal mystery from a variety of perspectives. Its aim has been to show the basis upon which a bold proclamation of this mystery depends. We have shown how the narrative of this mystery extends backward in time to Jesus' hidden life and public ministry and forward in time to the life and ministry of his body, the church. We have also shown how this mystery forms a part of what we have termed the metanarrative of God's economic plan of creation, redemption, and sanctification and how it originates from within the heart of the Trinity itself. We have demonstrated that this mystery touches every dimension of human existence and that it even has an effect on the way God chooses to relate to us. We have also shown that, through baptism, the narrative of the paschal mystery is now closely interwoven with our own.

In the final analysis, the paschal mystery belongs to Christ. It concerns the redemptive action of his passion, death, and resurrection, along with the many conditions that make this existential drama possible. On Easter morning, Christ announced his defeat of death by appearing to his disciples. They, in turn, provided the basic narrative key around which the entire gospel proclamation revolves: "He is risen!" Without Jesus' resurrection the paschal mystery collapses and, along with it, the entire gospel proclamation. Jesus' resurrection represents God's bold proclamation of his love for us. It keeps alive in us the hope that our final destiny lies in sharing in the intimate love of the Triune God. It invites us to open our hearts to God so that God might open his heart to us. When this mutual opening of hearts occurs, our lives can never be the same. The transformation it initiates in us touches every aspect of our being—and the heart of God, as well. Jesus' paschal mystery is our paschal mystery. We celebrate it whenever we gather together in his name, especially at the liturgy, when the redemptive action of Christ enters space and time and invites us to share more deeply in the intimate relations of the divine.

CHAPTER TWO

The Paschal Mystery in the Eucharistic Liturgy

The other sacraments, as well as every ministry of the Church and every work of the apostolate, are linked with the holy Eucharist and are directed toward it. For the most blessed Eucharist contains the Church's entire spiritual wealth, that is, Christ Himself, our Passover and living bread. Through His very flesh, made vital and vitalizing by the Holy Spirit, He offers life to men. They are thereby invited and led to offer themselves, their labors, and all created things together with Him.

Second Vatican Council
Presbyterorum ordinis, no. 5

Christ's paschal mystery touches us in a very personal way. It has become a part of our story, so much so that our lives make little sense apart from it. We share in it because we believe Christ is "the way, and the truth, and the life" (John 14:6). Christ is everything to us—or, at least, he should be. We share in his paschal mystery because we share in his life. Christian discipleship is not about following abstract truths or principles. It is all about a relationship to a living person, Jesus of Nazareth, who walked this earth some two thousand years ago and who walks it still today through the members of his body, the church. Our creed tells us that Jesus suffered, died, and was buried. It also affirms his resurrection from the dead, his ascension into heaven, and his coming in glory at the end of time to judge the living and the dead.[1] We must give more than mere intellectual assent to these truths of the faith, if we wish to enter into a personal relationship with Jesus. We must open our hearts to him and trust him with our hopes, our dreams, and our very lives.

As with any friendship, we must foster this relationship with Jesus. We have to talk to him, listen to him, and spend time with him. We need to do this both as a community and as individuals. The Christian liturgy gives us the opportunity to do so; it steeps us in Christ's paschal mystery and puts us in touch with the living God. Of all the liturgical rites and sacraments at our disposal, the Eucharist has particular significance for our daily lives. This "sacrament of the paschal mystery" rests in the heart of the church and stands at the center of its life.[2] When we celebrate it, the whole of Christ's paschal mystery becomes present to us. Much more takes place than a symbolic enactment of Jesus' Last Supper. As a sacrament of the church, the Eucharist puts us in close, personal contact with Jesus, the sacrament of God. Jesus enters our midst and touches us with the redemptive action of his passion, death, and resurrection.

The Liturgy and the Paschal Mystery

Christ's paschal mystery is central to God's plan for our salvation. It takes place both in and out of time and comes to us now primarily through the liturgy. This intimate connection between the paschal mystery and the liturgy touches the very heart of God's relationship with his people. The sacraments are visible, efficacious signs of Christ's redeeming love. Through them, he mediates his presence to us and immerses us in his paschal mystery.

One of the most eloquent and comprehensive descriptions of the paschal mystery and its vital relationship to the church's liturgy comes from Cyprian Vagaggini. He writes:

> The paschal mystery is the fact that Jesus is not only the incarnate Son of God, but incarnate and revealed *in forma servi,* and, what is more, dead and risen, the *Kyrios.* More precisely it is the fact that He, as *Kyrios,* is now seated at the right hand of the Father, in the continuous and glorious exercise, always as man, of His mediation as High Priest; and that, by means of His humanity, comprised in His glorious body, He communicates to us the divine life with which that body is not only full but even resplendent, the sole dispenser of divine life, allowing us primarily through the liturgy—and not only us but in some way the whole world—to pass over from spiritual and physical death to

total life in God. The ultimate end of this process activated by Him is to make us, body and soul, like Himself in death and resurrection, so that, having communicated insofar as is possible His same form of existence and of action to everyone who sincerely follows Him, and having instituted a new heaven and a new earth, He might be able to offer everything together with Himself to the Father, and that finally God might be all in all.[3]

The above passage offers in a precise and relatively compact form a sweeping vision of the central role of the paschal mystery in God's plan of salvation. It presents the paschal mystery as a fact, embracing both human and divine realities, with the specific goal of making all things new in Christ so that all of reality might be offered to God and so that God might be in all and for all. It affirms that Jesus became man and took on the form of a slave not only to save us from death, but also so that we might have an intimate share in God's life. It also states that, through his death, resurrection, and ascension to the right hand of the Father, Jesus is the sole dispenser of divine life and that he mediates that life to us through his divinized humanity, in his role as high priest primarily through the liturgy. The liturgy is the ordinary way God has provided for us to receive the divine life won for us through Christ's paschal mystery. God has given it to us so that during our historical sojourn we might have concrete, visible assurances of his presence in our midst. This presence is active, vital, and dynamic. Through the celebration of the liturgy, Christ enters our world yet again and gives himself completely, to the point of dying for us, so that he can become nourishment for us and a source of hope.

The question might arise concerning just how Christ acts through the church's celebration of the liturgy. As with any mystery, we cannot verify such an action empirically, but only affirm it with the conviction of faith. The faith of the church asserts that Christ is present in the liturgy in a variety of ways. As the fathers of the Second Vatican Council remind us:

To accomplish so great a work, Christ is always present in His Church, especially in her liturgical celebrations. He is present in the sacrifice of the Mass, not only in the person of His minister, "the same one now offering, through the ministry of priests, who formerly offered himself on the cross," but especially under the Eucharistic species. By His power He is present in the sacraments; so that when a man baptizes, it is really Christ Himself who baptizes. He is present in His word, since it is He Himself who speaks when the holy Scriptures are read in the church. He is present, finally, when the Church prays and sings, for He promised, "Where two or three are gathered together for my sake, there am I in the midst of them" (Mt 18:20).[4]

Through these multiple presences, Christ comes to his people and presents their prayers as his own to the Father. The Father, in turn, offers us through Christ's divinized humanity an intimate sharing in his life. We cannot explain how this occurs. We can only attest to what the church believes. The liturgy is central to that faith: "...every liturgical celebration, because it is an action of Christ the priest and of His body the Church, is a sacred action surpassing all others. No other action of the Church can match its claim to efficacy, nor equal the degree of it."[5]

Of all the church's liturgical celebrations, one in particular enjoys prominence of place because of its special relationship to the paschal mystery. The eucharistic sacrifice, we are told, "...is the fount and apex of the whole Christian life." Everything else in the church's life and ministry flows from it and is oriented toward it. It contains "...the Church's entire spiritual wealth, that is, Christ Himself, our Passover and living bread."[6] Just how does the Eucharist put us in touch with Christ's paschal mystery? Once again, we must rely on the testimony of the church's faith. To understand the relationship between the two, we need to look at the symbolic nature of Jesus' last meal with his disciples, its significance as a prophetic event at the close of his public ministry, and its important relationship to the events that followed.

The Eucharist and the Paschal Mystery[7]

Jesus' words of blessing on the evening before his death make little sense unless they are understood as a symbolic representation of a new covenant between God and humanity. The bread and wine he shares with his disciples signify the sacrifice of his body and blood to be given up and poured out for the sake of many. By placing his passion and death in the context of his last Passover meal, Jesus provides his followers with a concrete way of remembrance that exists in continuity with the tradition of their ancestors and that also raises their awareness of a new, definitive action of God in their lives. In this respect, it partakes in those very events that shape his own destiny in the plan of his Father.

Jesus' last meal is linked not only with the events following it, but also with those preceding it. In all three of the Synoptic Gospels, his public ministry both begins and ends with a symbolic action: the former, that of his baptism by John in the Jordan (Matt 3:13–17; Mark 1:9–11; Luke 3:21–22); the latter, that of the first Eucharist (Matt 26:26–29; Mark14:22–25; Luke 22:19–20). Even in the Gospel of John, which includes neither Jesus' baptism nor the actual words of institution, the account of his public ministry contains many allusions to the eucharistic banquet. These include changing the water into wine at Cana (2:1–12), the miracle of the loaves (6:1–15), his discourse at Capernaum (6:22–66, especially 32–58), the discourse on the vine and the branches (15:1–17), and the meal of bread and fish (21:9–14).[8] The point here is that, while Jesus' words of institution (considered authentic even according to the standards of biblical criticism) link the Last Supper with the events of his passion and death, the evangelists (writing under the inspiration of the Holy Spirit) associate it also with the events of his public ministry.[9] The Synoptic authors achieve the latter by using the symbolic actions of the Lord's baptism and Last Supper as a means of defining the limits of his public ministry; the author of the Gospel of John does so by filling the account of Jesus' ministry of teaching and healing with numerous eucharistic undertones. In this way, they connect the Eucharist as much to the life as to the death of the Lord Jesus. Moreover, in both cases, they point to what obviously stands out as the culminating event of his life and death, that is, his resurrection on Easter Sunday morning.

In his use of symbolism as a means of communicating the truth of his redemptive mission, Jesus stands in marked continuity with the long tradition of Hebrew prophetic utterance. Hosea's marriage to the faithless Gomer (Hos 1:2–9), Jeremiah's symbols of the loincloth (Jer 13:1–11) and the shattered wine jugs (12–14), Ezekiel's making of bread from a single pot of wheat, barley, beans, lentils, millet, and spelt (Ezek 4:9) and his mime of the emigrant (12:1–20) are all examples of the prophetic use of concrete material signs and

actions to convey the message of Yahweh to his people. When inter-
preting these actions, we can easily forget that, as authentic utter-
ances of the word of God, they actually bring into effect what they
symbolize: "[God's word] shall not return...empty" (Isa 55:11).[10]
Jesus' breaking of the bread and drinking from the cup in the com-
pany of his disciples brings the event of Calvary into their midst.
Before his actual death, he makes present the redemptive effects of
that first Good Friday in the bread and wine, which he eats and
drinks with his disciples. These effects culminate in his Easter rising
and, as stated earlier, are already anticipated in his ministry of teaching and healing.

The Church's Eucharistic Teaching

Jesus' institution of the Eucharist was rooted in this long tradition of Hebrew prophetic utterance. It took place in the context of a
sacred meal with his disciples, an action symbolizing his redemptive
suffering and death on the cross. Asked by Jesus to remember him in
this sacred action, his disciples and the communities established by
them came to see that the breaking of the bread involved: (1) a foretaste of the heavenly banquet, (2) the continuing presence of the
Risen Lord in their midst, and (3) the sacrificial reality of Christ's
redemptive death.[11] Disagreement over the precise nature of each of
these elements and the way in which they interact with one another
has been the cause of much unrest and turmoil in the history of the
church. The Catholic tradition affirms three fundamental truths. In
the words of John Paul II: "The mystery of the Eucharist—sacrifice,
presence, banquet—does not allow for reduction or exploitation; it
must be experienced and lived in its integrity, both in its celebration
and in the intimate converse with Jesus which takes place after
receiving communion or in a prayerful moment of Eucharistic adoration apart from mass."[12] Each of these elements is fundamental to
Catholic teaching.

The Eucharist as Banquet

Even to the external observer, the relationship that the Eucharist
has to the fellowship of a sacred meal is obvious and nearly always
presumed. Like the Passover—its Jewish counterpart—the celebration of the Eucharist commemorates the great saving acts of God on

behalf of his people. Its purpose is to bond Christians together, first through a telling of the great Christian narrative as it has been handed down through the gospels and interpreted by Paul and other apostolic witnesses of the faith, and then through the ritualistic sharing in the bread and cup, which Christ himself likened to the eating of his own body and blood. In this way, the Eucharist serves as a focus of identity for the Christian people. By remembering the stories and performing the actions that Jesus asked to be done in his memory, we find ourselves drawing closer to one another and thus able to build community in what, at times, appears to be the most unlikely of circumstances. As food for wayfaring pilgrims, the Eucharist provides spiritual strength and nourishment for our earthly pilgrimage in faith. As a foretaste of the heavenly banquet, it preserves the hope that the reign of God manifested in Christ will one day be fully realized in our lives.[13] It should not be surprising that the Eucharist, when considered as a meal or banquet, receives almost universal acclaim: Christians of all denominations affirm the importance of the great spiritual strength they receive from their gathering in fellowship around the table of the Lord.

The Eucharist as Presence

The gospel story of the road to Emmaus (Luke 24:13–35) affirms that the Risen Christ was present to his followers in numerous ways: in their walk along the road (24:15), in their discussion of recent events (24:16–24), in the explanation of the scriptures (24:25–27), and, most especially, "in the breaking of the bread" (24:30–31). The latter involves not only the presence of Jesus, but also a knowledge of this presence on the part of his disciples. This recognition comes in the eucharistic action (i.e., "the *breaking* of the bread") and signifies Christ's dynamic personal presence to the community of believers in their celebration of the great commemorative action of his redemptive love: in their remembering, believers recognize the very person of Christ in the midst of the sacramental action for which they are giving thanks.

Christ is present in similar ways even in today's eucharistic celebrations: in coming to and going forth; in the explanation of the scriptures; in the accompanying theological reflection; most especially, in the breaking of the bread. Within Catholic circles, a special reverence is given to the presence of Christ in the person of the priest, who consecrates the eucharistic species. Since Vatican II, emphasis has also been placed on the presence of Christ in the worshipping community. While these various presences of Christ in the liturgy do not exist in tension with each other in and of themselves, it is understandable that, for various reasons, persons or communities of differing spiritualities might wish to emphasize one mode of Christ's presence over another (e.g., his presence in the Word over his presence in the community). One of the identifying characteristics of the Roman Catholic Church is an august theological realism that insists with firm religious conviction that, in the eucharistic celebration, the bread and wine are actually changed into the body and blood of the Risen Lord. Since its inception in the twelfth century, the term *transubstantiation* has gained the widest acceptance in Catholic circles to describe this transformation. As with all theological terms, however, it too is limited by the capacity of the philosophical assumptions supporting it, in this case the Aristotelian notions of substance and attribute. While the tradition must remain open to new possibilities for expressing the mystery of the transformation taking place during the words of consecration, it must also be aware of the philosophical limitations that any new formulation will necessarily bring with it.[14] Special care, moreover, must be taken not to discard a well-tried formulation solely in the name of theological experimentation. To be sure, it would be much more useful to the church if we were to view new formulations in conjunction with the old, being aware at all times, of course, of the various philosophical limitations of each, and of the particular beliefs that each, in its own time, originally intended to negate. In this way, we would not limit the mystery of the Eucharist to the assumptions of any one philosophical school or theological formulation.

The Eucharist as Sacrifice

When discussing the way in which the eucharistic celebration participates in the sacrifice on Calvary, the tendency in Catholic circles has been to emphasize the eternal aspect of Christ's redemptive act and its ability to enter the realm of history in whatever manner and whatever moment in time. Hence, we understand the origin of the well-known phrase: "The bloody sacrifice of Calvary is made present in the Mass in an unbloody way."[15] The great strength of such an expression is that it joins the action of the Mass to Christ's sacrifice on the cross without turning the former into a historical reenactment of the latter. Despite the accusations of the sixteenth-century reformers, the Catholic position has always affirmed the unique, unrepeatable nature of the event of Calvary. In fact, it is precisely because Christ's death extends beyond the bounds of time that it may now be invoked at any point along the continuum of history. Rather than a reenactment of Calvary, the celebration of the Eucharist is a sacramental realization of what, by all counts, is the veritable culmination of the whole of salvation history. Indeed, what needs to be brought out more in the discussion of the sacrificial aspects of the Eucharist is the way in which Christ's redemptive offering on Calvary is made present not only in its reality as an event, but also in the two conditions relating to it by way of cause and effect, that is, the incarnation and the resurrection. This is to say, the redemptive truth of Christ's bloody death presupposes both the reality of his becoming a man (the former could not have existed without the latter) and its causal relationship to his being raised on Easter morning by the power of the Father. In this respect, the contours of Christ's redemption of humanity encompass his entire life— from the manger to the empty tomb—and are made present substantially in the church's celebration of the Eucharist.[16] In the dramatic action of every Mass, Christ's becoming man, his dying on the cross, and his rising from the dead engage all who partake of the bread that is his body and the wine that is his blood. It is in receiving the body and blood of the Risen Lord in the eucharistic species that we receive the effects of Christ's redemptive action and are able to carry on his ministry of healing and teaching.[17] In this way, the Eucharist makes the paschal event present throughout the centuries. Through it, "...there is a truly enormous 'capacity' which embraces all of history as the recipient of the grace of redemption."[18]

Theological Corollaries

A number of important insights flow from these basic teachings. In the first place, the mystery of the Eucharist is not bound by the capacity of the philosophical and theological concepts that seek to penetrate its meaning. While a particular doctrinal formulation (including the present one) may be defined as an orthodox expression of the church's teaching, it could never be said to exhaust the full meaning of the mystery itself. In this regard, the church must be ever aware of new ways of understanding the mystery of Christ's action in the breaking of the bread and the drinking of the cup, while, at the same time, paying heed to those well-tried formulas that have served it well in the authentic proclamation of the faith.[19]

Second, while the Risen Christ is present to the church in any number of ways, he is recognized by its members most profoundly "in the breaking of the bread." The Eucharist is thus the center of the church's life—the point around which all else revolves. It is when celebrating this sacrament that the church is at home and most itself. Deprived of this special source of strength and spiritual sustenance, the church would find it difficult, if not impossible, to survive.[20]

Third, although it is primarily a communal celebration, the Eucharist can nurture (and, indeed, cannot do without) an intense private devotion. The relationship between the individual and communal dimensions of the sacrament should be understood as inclusive and mutually affirming. That is to say, the Eucharist can truly be a communal celebration only if the individuals forming a part of the celebration receive an internal affirmation of the reality and importance of their own personal relationship with the Risen Christ. Private devotions, in turn, are significant in that they give the individual a deeper awareness of the mystery of Christ's redemptive presence and action in the eucharistic celebration. While tensions are bound to exist, the overall relationship between private and communal devotion should be one that ultimately gives rise to balanced spiritual growth.[21]

Fourth, as grains of wheat are kneaded into a single loaf and as grapes are pressed and fermented into wine, so, too, the Eucharist draws individuals from different walks of life and transforms them into a unified body of believers. As the source of Christian unity, the Eucharist affirms the relation of harmony that should exist between believers. To receive the Eucharist in the midst of interior division of soul (i.e., personal sin) or exterior division in the family, community, or society at large (i.e., social sin) denigrates the worth of Christ's sacred action and trivializes the mystery for which it stands. This is true especially in the case of that false irenicism that often exists in the mutual relationships between the Catholic Church and its Protestant brothers and sisters.[22]

Fifth, as a foretaste of the heavenly banquet, the eucharistic celebration realizes the reign of God for the few moments during which the consecrated species has been received by and remains with the worshipping community. It thus manifests the eschatological orientation of God's people who, through their reception of the Eucharist, anticipate the full establishment of God's reign of peace and justice at the consummation of time. In this respect, the Eucharist gives us a glimpse of the happiness in God that they were intended from all eternity to possess.[23]

Finally, as already implied in the statement that Christ's redemptive action in the breaking of the bread is present in its cause (i.e., the incarnation), its reality (i.e., Calvary), and its effects (i.e., the Risen Lord), the Eucharist is related to the whole of theology. This is to say that Christ is just as much the Lord of theology as he is the Lord of history, and that there exists a particular eucharistic dimension to every theological discipline—dogma, moral, ascetical, mystical, as well as sacramental and liturgical. In this respect, the Eucharist provides a way of looking at the various disciplines of theology that promises to unify what all too often appears to be a field of unrelated enterprises with little bearing on life as it is really lived.[24]

This presentation of the Catholic teaching on the Eucharist, along with some basic theological corollaries, provides us with a useful background against which we can examine our actual experience of what happens when we gather for "the breaking of the bread." Discrepancies between what we are taught about the Eucharist, how we celebrate it, and how we actually experience it must be taken into account in a thorough discussion of its relation to Christ's paschal mystery.

Celebrating the Eucharist

Lex orandi, lex credendi, lex agendi.[25]

There exists an intimate connection between how the church prays, what it believes, and how it acts. This continuity between worship and the life of faith and morals has particular significance for the church's celebration of the Eucharist. When we gather to share in the breaking of the bread, the prayers we use to celebrate the sacrament say something significant about what we believe about the paschal mystery and the way it should influence our lives. Even a general look at the prayers of the church's eucharistic celebration bears this out.

Introductory Rites

A typical Sunday Mass begins with a series of Introductory Rites, the purpose of which is to gather the people of God together and prepare them for what is about to happen. These rites include an entrance song and procession, a greeting by the main celebrant, a penitential rite, the Kyrie, a Gloria, and an opening prayer. There is a significant amount of choice in the prayers in these opening rites. While they may vary slightly from one liturgical season to the next (e.g., there is no Gloria during Advent or Lent), their general purpose is to initiate the worship of the believing community. This worship takes place through Christ, in the Spirit, and for the Father.[26]

Taken together, these rites emphasize certain traits of the believing community that has gathered for worship. For one thing, they signify the unity of God's people. While it is true that we come to the celebration as individuals with our own needs and purposes, we gather in one place to unite ourselves in prayer with the church universal, both living and dead. The opening song and procession remind us that, when we gather for Eucharist, time and space become sacred for us. They also help us to recognize our bonds with the universal body of believers and with all of humanity. Gathered as God's people, the priest invites us to express our relationship to God not only as God's creatures but, because of the redemptive action of Christ that we are about to celebrate, also as God's adopted sons and daughters. The penitential rite helps us to get in touch with our sinful humanity, a reality that touches us as individuals, as a community, and as an entire race. Being aware of our sinfulness before God helps us to appreciate all that God has achieved for us in Christ. This awareness leads us to offer glory to God the Father, God the Son, and God the Holy Spirit and to extend a greeting of peace to all of God's people on earth. The opening collect gathers the prayers of the community in a single voice, directs those prayers to God, and prepares the community for their attentive listening to God's Word.

These Introductory Rites take place with the entire congregation standing, a posture that symbolizes the pilgrim nature of the worshipping community and that reminds the parish community that they are "sojourners in a foreign land."[27] Those involved in the procession—the alter servers, the lectors, the eucharistic ministers, the deacon, the priest and/or bishop—demonstrate by their movement through the congregation and into the sanctuary that the goal of the earthly pilgrimage of God's people is intimacy with the divine. This pilgrimage becomes possible through the mediation of Jesus Christ, which goes two ways: from the human to the divine and from the divine to the human. As such, it emphasizes not only the pilgrim nature of God's people, but also the pilgrim nature of God. We are able to journey to God only because God has decided to empty himself of his divinity and journey to us. Christ's paschal mystery lies at the very heart of this journey. He entered our world and gave of himself completely to the point of dying for us, so that he could become nourishment for us and a source of hope. These Introductory Rites also invite us to enter into our worship of God with every aspect of our being. The believing community gathers and expresses itself through song, movement, visible signs, heartfelt sentiments, thoughtful prayers, and silence. It does so because it recognizes that Jesus has come to redeem every aspect of our human makeup. At baptism, Christ immerses each of us in his paschal mystery. We gather at Eucharist to celebrate our ongoing participation in Christ's redeeming love and be renewed through our contact with it in the breaking of the bread.

The Liturgy of the Word

When the Introductory Rites are over, the community of believers sits for the Liturgy of the Word. At the Sunday liturgy, there normally are three readings: one from the Old Testament (or from the Acts of the Apostles during Easter time), one from the New Testament (usually from the Epistles or the Acts of the Apostles), and one from one of the four gospels. Between the first and second readings comes a responsorial psalm, which is recited or sung in an appropriate liturgical manner. In every season outside Lent, an alleluia verse is normally sung before the gospel. During Lent, however, a gospel acclamation takes the place of the alleluia. Following the gospel, there comes a homily and then a profession of faith and a series of general intercessions.[28]

People with specifically assigned ministries perform each part of the Liturgy of the Word. Lectors are responsible for the first two readings and the general intercessions; cantors are responsible for chanting the responsorial psalm and alleluia verse; a priest or deacon normally proclaims the gospel reading, preaches the homily, and introduces and closes the general intercessions. These assigned roles underscore the sacred nature of God's Word and the importance of proclaiming it in an appropriate manner. Each minister seeks to carry out his or her assigned ministry reverently and with competence. Each is encouraged to look upon his or her contribution as part of a larger whole, during which time Christ himself speaks to the believing community and encourages the people to walk a little bit further along the way of conversion.

This part of the Sunday liturgy offers the community of believers a time to listen to God speaking to them through the proclamation of the Word. It presupposes a dynamic, living faith, one that is willing both to listen intently to the message proclaimed and to take appropriate steps to implement it in one's daily life. For this to happen, however, much more is required than merely having competently trained ministers of the Word who can make the words of scripture come alive and preach with intellectual honesty and heartfelt conviction the good news of Jesus Christ to those present. In addition to this very important contribution, we, the members of the community, must cultivate the art of active listening that enables us to open our hearts, receive Christ's message, and embrace it as part of our own identity. In addition to such active listening, we also need to foster in our lives appropriate ways of translating what we have heard into a concrete response that has relevance for our immediate lives. Each of us has a responsibility for listening to God's Word and proclaiming it in our daily lives. Since the Liturgy of the Word belongs to the entire community, each of us has a responsibility to nurture that Word within our hearts, in our immediate vocational context (e.g., in the family and in the work place), and in the larger community.

The Liturgy of the Word helps us to interpret our present experience against the backdrop of salvation history. Such is the reason for the readings from the Old and New Testaments and for the prominence given to the gospel proclamation and to the exposition of the readings given in the homily. Christ's paschal mystery represents the fullness of God's salvific action on behalf of his people. The Liturgy of the Word seeks to break open the words of scripture so that we might be able to understand the ways in which we participate in that mystery today, in the circumstances of daily life. As a believing community, we are called to be a people of the Word. God's Word is living and effective: it accomplishes what it sets out to do and does not return in vain. The Liturgy of the Word seeks to help us to open our hearts to God's Word so that it might take root there and be born within us. In doing so, it affirms our identity as members of Christ's body and readies us for the even deeper participation in Christ's paschal mystery that is about to take place.

The Liturgy of the Eucharist

After the Liturgy of the Word, the community remains seated for the beginning of the Liturgy of the Eucharist. This part of the Mass contains three main elements: The Preparation of the Gifts, the Eucharistic Prayer, and the Communion Rite. Each of these forms an integral part of the Liturgy of the Eucharist.

During the Preparation of the Gifts, the congregation remains seated, while the Lord's table is prepared with the necessary implements (e.g., corporal, purificator, missal, chalice), the gifts of bread and wine are brought to the altar (often in procession), and the priest readies the gifts by offering them to God in the name of Christ and on behalf of the believing community. During this time, an appropriate song is often sung to prepare the people's hearts for the sacrificial offering that is about to take place. This opening rite of the Liturgy of the Eucharist has a twofold purpose: it provides an appropriate transition from the Liturgy of the Word to the second part of the Mass; and it readies the community both materially and spiritually for the central part of the Liturgy of the Eucharist.[29]

This central part takes place during the eucharistic prayer and contains eight main elements, during which time we express ourselves together through reverential postures (e.g., standing and/or kneeling). First, there is a Preface, or prayer of thanksgiving, when the priest prays on our behalf and gives thanks to God the Father for the work of salvation. Then comes the *Sanctus* or "Holy, Holy," which acclaims the glory and holiness of the God of heaven and earth and of the one who comes in his name. This acclamation is followed by the *Epiclesis,* when the church asks God through the prayers of the celebrant to send his Spirit upon the gifts of bread and wine so that they might become the body and blood of Christ. This prayer is followed by the Institution narrative and consecration. Here, the priest recalls the words of Jesus at the Last Supper when he offered, under the appearances of bread and wine, his body and blood to his apostles to eat and commanded them to carry on this mystery.

The consecration of the bread and wine is then followed by the *Anamnesis,* when the church recalls the relationship of the Eucharist to Jesus' passion, resurrection, and ascension. This memorial is followed by an Offering, when the church offers Jesus' consecrated body and blood to the Father and the Holy Spirit as a spotless victim offered for the sins of many. During this time, we offer ourselves with Christ and rely on his mediation for a deeper and more intimate union with the Father and with one another. Intercessions follow that unite us with the universal church and ask God to give all the faithful, both living and dead, a share in the new life that has been purchased for them by Christ's body and blood. The Eucharistic Prayer ends with a *final doxology* that gives honor and glory to God, the Almighty Father. This Final Prayer is made through Christ, with Christ, in Christ, and in the unity of the Holy Spirit.

These eight prayers are intimately related and represent the dynamic action of Christ made through and on behalf of the members of his body, the church. While the Institution narrative and consecration stand out as the most important elements of the Eucharistic Prayer, we should not view them in isolation from the other parts. The Eucharistic Prayer is Christ's prayer to the Father. Because it is his prayer, it is also the prayer of the members of his body, the church. Each element of this prayer is important and forms an intimate part in the mediation performed by Christ on our behalf.[30]

The Communion Rite focuses on the Eucharist as a paschal meal. We stand and pray the Lord's Prayer together, presenting God the Father with our various needs, especially that of receiving our daily bread. This prayer is followed by a Rite of Peace, which celebrates the unity of the church made possible by Christ's paschal mystery and points to the peace of the kingdom that takes place at the eschatological banquet of which the Eucharist is foretaste. After we have exchanged signs of peace, the priest breaks the bread and drops a piece of it into the chalice of wine to represent the mingling of Jesus' body and blood. As this takes place, we sing or recite the *Lamb of God,* an invocation that asks Jesus, "the Lamb of God who takes away the sins of the world," to "grant us peace." Following this invocation, the priest prepares himself for his own communion, then presents the consecrated body and blood of Christ to us, and then distributes communion. During the distribution of communion, we process as a body to symbolize our unity as the people of God. To make this unity even more pronounced, a song is often sung to display a union in spirit through the unity of our voices. After communion, we spend some time sitting in silence to reflect upon the gift we have just received and to thank God for our sharing in Christ's Pasch. A meditation song is sometimes used to help us express our grateful sentiments to God. There follows a concluding prayer where the priest asks God to bring fruitful effects from the mystery just celebrated. We make this prayer our own by responding, "Amen."[31]

The Liturgy of the Eucharist brings Christ's paschal mystery to the believing community. It does so by making the mystery of Jesus' passion, death, resurrection, and ascension present through visible signs specifically instituted by Christ to commemorate his passage from death to life. What happens at the Liturgy of the Eucharist is more than a mere symbolic reenactment. The fullness of Christ's paschal mystery becomes present in a mystical way. As members of Christ's body, we celebrate the Liturgy of the Eucharist not only so that it might become present to us, but also so that we might become present to it. The narrative of Jesus' paschal mystery has now become our own. What the Liturgy of the Word has prepared us for through the retelling of incidents from salvation history the Liturgy of the Eucharist now makes manifest to us in a real and substantial way. The word of God prepares our hearts to receive the body and blood of Jesus our Pasch. Once we have received Jesus in this way, our story becomes more deeply interwoven with his. The Liturgy of the Eucharist *is* Christ's paschal mystery. Its unique characteristic is that it mediates this mystery to us today in a concrete, visible way. As a result, we are able to share more deeply in Christ's redeeming love and work for the establishment of his kingdom in the world we live in.

Concluding Rite

After the Liturgy of the Eucharist, the Mass comes to a close with a short Concluding Rite. The priest invites us to stand for prayer and addresses us with the short greeting, "The Lord be with you." We respond in kind with, "And also with you." He then blesses us in the name of the Father, Son, and Spirit and dismisses us. On special occasions the blessing can be longer and more solemn. If present, a deacon dismisses us. After these final words, a hymn is normally sung as the priest, deacon, and other ministers process out of the sanctuary. As in the Introductory Rites, their closing procession represents the people of God on their pilgrim journey through life.[32]

This Concluding Rite brings closure to the eucharistic celebration. It is much shorter than the Introductory Rites, because its focus is not on what has just taken place, but on the loving witness we are called to give to others when we leave. The Mass is over, but the celebration of the Eucharist is meant to continue in our lives as it is manifested in our good works and loving consideration of others. There is an intimate bond between the eucharistic celebration and leading an authentic Christian life. Those of us participating in the Eucharist must strive to make what we celebrate in church a reality in our everyday lives. We do so by taking the last words of the priest or deacon to heart: "The Mass is ended. Go in peace to love and to serve the Lord." As we leave our celebration, we continue giving thanks to God for all that he has done for us. We praise the Lord and bless his name by striving to live our lives in conformity with the gospel. Christ's paschal mystery has come to us. We now seek to bring it to others by the powerful witness of lives sincerely dedicated to the service of others.

Observations

The above presentation of the eucharistic celebration and its relationship to Christ's paschal mystery has important repercussions for the Christian spiritual moral life. The following remarks pertain to our perceptions and motivations when we come to Mass and when we leave it. They focus on what the prayers of the Mass intend to convey, how we perceive them, and what behaviors they actually reinforce.

1. On the most fundamental level, it is important for us to recognize that our presence at the eucharistic celebration must stem from a free and unimpeded decision to participate in and share in the fruits of Christ's paschal mystery. Going to Mass on Sunday is not just another weekly activity placed on a par with all the others that take up our time and crowd our busy schedules. It is the most important thing we do all week and should be looked upon and treated as such. We need to have our awareness raised about the significance of our participation in the Eucharist for our daily lives. In the past, we have often considered our participation in terms of obligation and the penalty of sin for not attending. We need to emphasize more the benefits received from attending the eucharistic celebration rather than what will happen to us if we fail to attend. The nourishment we receive from it is unique. We are only kidding ourselves if we think otherwise. We attend Sunday Mass, however, not only to receive, but primarily to give. The eucharistic celebration is a time of praise and thanksgiving. We gather to unite our prayers to Christ's in a communal action of adoration, praise, and thanksgiving to the Father. We are able to pray in this way only because Christ has made it possible for us to do so by virtue of his passion, death, resurrection, and ascension to the right hand of the Father. It is very important that we be aware of the decision we make to participate in the eucharistic liturgy. Sometimes this decision is difficult to make. Sometimes we do not wish to attend. Sometimes we can think of a host of reasons for not going. Our decision to attend the Sunday liturgy stems from the decision of discipleship, the desire to follow Jesus through thick and thin, to have our lives become more deeply intertwined with his. Our participation at the Sunday Eucharist enables this deeper participation in Christ's paschal mystery to take place. Our experience of all that happens during it needs to be understood against this underlying decision of discipleship. Without it, the Sunday Eucharist can turn into nothing but an empty, meaningless ritual with little (if any) impact on our daily lives.

2. At the same time, we must also recognize that there is (and will probably always be) a gap between the vision presented to us by the various prayers of the eucharistic celebration and our actual experience of them. Despite our best intentions, we never leave all

of our cares and concerns behind when we attend Sunday Mass—nor should we. As Saint Augustine has said, we are citizens of two worlds, "the city of God and the city of man."[33] We are a pilgrim people with one foot in each of these worlds. The purpose of the eucharistic celebration is not to take us out of the world and transport us to another world of divine origin. It can only give us a taste of what we are called to become and then direct us back to our situation in the world in order to be instruments of change for the sake of God's kingdom. We come to the Eucharist as a body of believers, conscious of our sinful humanity, yet filled with the hope that Christ's paschal mystery will immerse us in the Father's love and eventually overcome our sinfulness. The gap between the vision the eucharistic celebration presents to us and the reality of our broken and sinful humanity should put us in touch with our need for conversion. Our participation in the Eucharist is not some magic elixir that will instantly solve our problems with little or no effort on our part. We participate in the Eucharist as members of Christ's body, conscious of God's presence in our lives, yet painfully aware of the call Christ extends to us to follow in his footsteps. If Christ's paschal mystery is truly shaping our lives, then we should fully expect periods of darkness and intense suffering during our earthly sojourn. Only by experiencing the pain and suffering that Christ experienced during his time of passion can we expect to rise above it and to share in the new life that his resurrection from the dead promises us. When faced with the discrepancy between vision and reality during our eucharistic celebration, the key question is not whether the gap exists, but whether it is gradually diminishing over time. Our immersion in Christ's paschal mystery at the Sunday liturgy has much to do with where we are along the way of conversion. Those who gather for a typical Sunday Mass will experience it in a multitude of ways. Regardless of how they experience it, however, the reality of Christ's paschal mystery will be present and extend the invitation to them to participate in and be shaped by the ongoing action of Christ's redeeming love.

3. Those who gather for the Sunday Liturgy should also be encouraged to look upon what takes place there as a single, integral action of the local community in union with the church universal. The Eucharist is not a private devotion or a collection of actions of varying importance. From beginning to end, the entire celebration is

an action of Christ and should be understood and looked upon in this way. In the past, we have often looked to the words of institution as the essence of the Mass, while everything else was of less importance. While the institution narrative and the words of consecration represent the culmination of Christ's eucharistic action, they must be seen in the context of the entire ritual. As in any celebration, the Eucharist has its rituals of welcoming, reflection, joyous expression, and departure. The various parts of the Mass—from the Introductory to the Concluding Rites—accomplish these ends and, in doing so, make important statements about our own self-understanding. We need to look upon the Sunday Mass as a time when we gather to celebrate Christ's paschal mystery and make a statement about our own participation in it. To celebrate the paschal mystery in an appropriate manner and to appreciate our close relationship to it, we look upon it as a single dramatic action. In this way, we will better understand the varying presences of Christ in the liturgy. Christ is present to us as we gather as members of his body to celebrate his paschal mystery. He is present to us when we hear the word of God proclaimed and reflect upon its meaning for our lives. He is present to us when we gather around the table of the Lord and commemorate the supper he celebrated with us and left us as a memorial of his Easter Pasch. He is present to us as we process up to the altar to receive his body and blood. He is present to us as we sit in silence in the unity of the Spirit that the breaking of the bread has unleashed in our hearts, and he is present as the priest and those with him process out at the end of Mass and as we join them when we leave our pews and go our separate ways. During the eucharistic celebration Christ's actions are deeply interwoven with our own. These many actions form the drama of his paschal mystery, which, through our participation in the Mass, becomes the drama of our daily lives.

4. For this to happen, however, we must fully recognize what the drama of Christ's paschal mystery proposes to do for us. The Mass celebrates the paschal mystery as a living reality, as an event that takes place and, in some mysterious way, becomes present to those who participate in the commemoration of the Lord's last meal with his disciples. Although rooted in a specific moment in history, Christ's paschal mystery transcends time and communes with the eternal. Through the Eucharist, it reaches down from eternity and

enters our world so that the effects of Christ's redemptive action can touch our lives in the present moment. The Eucharist provides God's people with a visible, concrete means for the paschal mystery to enter our world and provide us with the salvation bought for us by Christ through his passion, death, and resurrection. This sacramental action is the ordinary means through which God's people have access to Christ's redemptive action. Without it, there would be no established way for us to get in touch with the paschal mystery today. The Eucharist is the source and center of the Christian life precisely because it brings Christ's paschal mystery into our midst wherever and whenever we celebrate it. It receives its very identity from Christ's paschal mystery and is completely at one with his ongoing redemptive action. When we celebrate the Eucharist, we not only receive the benefits of Christ's paschal mystery, but also become active participants in it. What Jesus experienced through his passion, death, and resurrection continues to take place in the members of his body. Our participation in this redemptive action forms us into the likeness of Christ, who emptied himself of his divinity and became one of us so that we might enjoy the rewards of eternal life. We celebrate the Eucharist to affirm our belief in what Christ has done for us and in what he continues to do through us. We go to Mass on Sunday to profess our faith in the power of Christ's transforming love. We derive our identity from what we celebrate. The Eucharist affirms us and tells us who we are: the people of God, members of his body, disciples called to follow him and to serve him—wherever he may lead.

5. When considered an integral part of the eucharistic celebration, the Introductory Rites prepare us for this deeper participation in Christ's paschal mystery. They do so by gathering us together as God's people, by helping us to get in touch with our sinful humanity, and by offering glory and praise to Jesus our Resurrected Lord. These rites help us to ready ourselves for the celebration ahead. They do so, however, not by separating us from daily life, but by inviting us to look at it from a much deeper perspective. They remind us of our common humanity, our sinful humanity, and the new humanity we share through Christ Jesus. As such, they emphasize the continuity that already exists between the lives we are trying to live as followers of Christ and the mystery about to be celebrated that makes such a following possible. They offer us a moment of reflection, a time

when we put aside the hectic pace of daily life in order to get in touch with the great themes of Christ's paschal narrative. Already, at the very outset of the Mass, these themes make their way to the forefront of our common awareness. They remind us of the values of human solidarity, of human frailty, and of human redemption. These are the reasons why we gather as a people, ask God's forgiveness for our faults and failings, and offer glory and praise to Jesus, "the Lamb of God who takes away the sin of the world." These are the reasons why we gather to celebrate the mystery of Christ's Easter Pasch. The Introductory Rites call us out of life and into a deeper celebration of life. They ready us for our entrance into the defining event of human history and of all creation—the passion, death, and resurrection of Jesus Christ. As we celebrate these rites, we affirm both the historical and the transcendent nature of this event. Christ's paschal mystery has already taken place and accomplished its purpose. If it did not, we would not be able to gather as God's people and give glory and praise to our Risen Lord. At the same time, our experience of our sinful humanity reminds us that the full effects of Christ's redemptive action have not yet permeated our lives and that we must wait with hopeful longing for the coming of his kingdom. We celebrate the Eucharist to allow Christ's paschal mystery to enter our lives and to keep alive in us the hope that all of Christ's promises to us will come to fulfillment.

6. With the Liturgy of the Word, we find ourselves immersed in the great narrative of salvation history. The readings and psalms selected for the day represent only a part of this larger narrative, all of which is moving toward a dramatic climax in Christ's paschal history. The Liturgy of the Word invites us to look upon our own history as individuals and as a people against the backdrop of the history of God's salvific plan for humanity. We participate in this part of the Mass by actively listening to the readings and by pondering their significance for our lives. The homily's purpose is to facilitate this process of self-reflection, not to take its place. A good homily leaves us with something to think about that relates directly to our attitudes, values, and daily actions. During the Liturgy of the Word, we celebrate God's Word to humanity; we celebrate our capacity to hear it and reflect upon it. Most of all, we celebrate our ability to respond to it. All of these activities take place under the influence of God's Spirit, who inspires those involved—lectors, cantors, homilist, and

the faithful—to proclaim God's Word and receive it in their heart's inner sanctum. Christ's paschal mystery is the major focus of this proclamation and reception of God's Word. It provides the community with the hermeneutical key that unlocks the mysteries of God's revelation to his people. It sheds light on all of God's revelation to humanity that took place both before Christ's coming and after it. It inspires those gathered to proclaim their fundamental tenets of their faith with renewed vigor and it leads them to offer up heartfelt petitions for the church, the world, and for all those in need. Most of all, it orients the proclamation of God's Word toward the Liturgy of the Eucharist that is about to take place. It does so by bringing to the fore the central role the Christ event plays in the entire history of salvation. This focus on Christ ultimately leads the community of those gathered to celebrate his presence in their midst. As members of his body, we come to recognize that God's Word is also our own. At the Liturgy of the Word, we hear it proclaimed and receive it into our hearts, so that we might proclaim it in our lives with words and actions of our own making.

7. With the Liturgy of the Eucharist, we do not merely recount the event of Christ's paschal mystery; it actually enters our midst. During its celebration, this event becomes present to the believing community in a very specific way. We are not passive onlookers who merely watch the paschal mystery as it unfolds before us. As members of Christ's body, we now are active participants in this event. Although Christ is the primary actor in this dramatic unfolding of the paschal mystery before our eyes, he speaks and acts through the words and actions of the priest, the deacon, other ministers of the eucharistic assembly, and the community of those gathered. Through the paschal mystery, Christ has united his humanity to our own. At the Liturgy of the Eucharist, Christ acts in and through our ritual commemoration of his passion, death, and resurrection. He presides over the Eucharist as *Kyrios,* the Resurrected Lord sitting at the right hand of the Father. United with him, we offer the various prayers of the Eucharist to God, the Father. We do so as God's adopted sons and daughters redeemed by Christ's act of selfless love. The Liturgy of the Eucharist gives us a time to have fellowship with Christ and one another. It allows us to celebrate his presence in our midst, most especially in the eucharistic species of bread and wine transformed into his body and blood. It immerses us in the action of his sacrifi-

cial death and enables us to rise with him to new life as members of his body and as a part of a new creation. Because of our participation in the Eucharist, our lives can no longer remain the same. Our participation in Christ's paschal mystery changes our perspective. It gives us a different way of looking at life. We sense that our actions are no longer entirely our own. We discover that we are part of a larger body, a universal community that lives out its life in close communion with the Resurrected Lord. We celebrate the Liturgy of the Eucharist as gift and thanksgiving. It offers us food for our journey through life and drink that refreshes us with new and deeper insights into the mystery of who we are and what we are destined to become. It brings Christ and his paschal mystery into our midst and seals our identity with his. Everything good in our lives is made possible by this close alignment with Christ. His life, death, resurrection, and ascension into heaven give our lives meaning and strength. Jesus is our reconciliation with the Father; his paschal mystery has made this reconciliation possible. It is for this reason that we give heartfelt thanks to God.

8. With the Concluding Rite, the believing community looks back on what it has just celebrated. It also looks forward to carrying out its mission of leading dedicated lives of service. Just as the Introductory Rites provide a transition for the daily life of the community to its celebration of Christ's paschal mystery, so does the Concluding Rite offer a transition in the other direction. The purpose of this closing ritual is not to set up a wall between the community's liturgical worship and daily life, but to emphasize the continuity between the two. We celebrate the Eucharist not to escape from life, but in order to embrace its challenges with more rigor and deeper dedication. The Concluding Rite sends us back into the world. Wherever we go and whatever we do, it asks us to carry the Lord with us so that we might love and serve him. In doing so, it makes a very concrete statement about the nature of Christ's paschal mystery. It reminds us that Christ continues to live and love, to suffer, rise, and die in those who serve him. It reminds us that we, the community of believers, have dedicated ourselves to following him. It reminds us of the call of discipleship and asks us not to count the cost. When we leave Mass, our thoughts should be on those we have been called to serve. More often than not, these people are in close physical proximity to us. They are our family members, neighbors,

and co-workers. They are the poor and those in need in our local community. They are those who need our help—of whatever kind—but are either too proud or hesitant to ask for it. We leave church on Sunday to carry on Christ's mission in our little corner of the world. We, the community of believers, are the local church. We are Christ's arms and legs in this particular locale at this particular juncture in history. Today, at this particular moment in space and time, Christ touches others through our kindness, through our consideration, through our compassion. His paschal mystery is not limited to the eucharistic celebration itself. It bursts into our lives and, through us, into the lives of those we touch.

9. The challenge before the believing community each time it gathers for Eucharist is to look at this celebration as a source of life and nourishment. It must do so even when it finds a gap between the vision presented in the prayers of the liturgy and what it actually experiences. This is especially important given the wide range of age groups normally present at a typical parish Sunday celebration and the varying levels of psychological and faith development. It is extremely difficult (and rare) for everyone present at the Eucharist to experience the Mass at the same level and degree of intensity. Nor is this to be expected. Different members bring different gifts. The body of Christ does not have a homogeneous experience of Christ's presence in its midst. Our God is a God of surprises. God works wonders in our midst in and through the variety of his members, regardless of their level of psychological or spiritual maturity. The Christian community gathers for Eucharist to allow God to be God in their lives. Because of Christ's paschal mystery, God comes to us and meets us where we are. He searches *us* out—not vice versa. There is no need for us to go on a long, unending search for him. Jesus is Emmanuel, "God-with-us." His paschal mystery reveals the depths of his love for us. It also provides us with the opportunity to demonstrate the depths of our love for him. Jesus accepts whatever we are able to offer him and then presents it to his Father. He meets us where we are and then, through the influence of his Spirit, gently nudges us along the way of conversion. The discrepancy between vision and reality confronting our experience ultimately represents a challenge of faith. Jesus himself said, "Blessed are those who have not seen and yet have come to believe" (John 20:29). Our celebration of the Eucharist is a testament to our faith. We do not see that what we pro-

claim is taking place. At times, it may even be difficult for us to believe that Christ and his paschal mystery are truly present in our midst. In today's world, faith and doubt often exist side by side in both our heads and our hearts. We should not allow this to distract us. Jesus himself is aware of our situation. He himself will narrow the gap between vision and reality. He himself will deepen our faith. He himself will meet us where we are, show us what we are called to become, and gently lead us there.

10. Finally, the Eucharist, as Christ's Easter Pasch, addresses every level of our human makeup: the physical, the emotional, the intellectual, the spiritual, the social, and the universal. It does so not only because each of these dimensions finds expression in our common worship, but also because they are lifted up through Christ and in him have been and are in the process of becoming thoroughly redeemed. When we gather for Eucharist, we offer our humanity to the Father in union with Christ's humanity. This union is not a superficial juxtaposition of opposites, but an intimate mingling of the old humanity with the new. Christ has become like us in all things except sin (cf. Heb 4:15). He became human in order that we might become divine.[34] He conquered sin and death by means of his cross and resurrection and now unites us to himself so that we might do the same. The Eucharist marks this movement in our lives. Through it, we immerse ourselves in Christ's paschal mystery, confront the realities of sin and death in our lives, and overcome them. We can do so only because of Christ's paschal mystery. What he has done, he also promises to do in us. We are able to follow him not so much out of our love for him, but because of his love for us. Jesus is at work in our lives despite our stubbornness and contrary tendencies. Through his passion, death, and resurrection, he recreates our sinful and broken humanity and unites it to his own. With him as our guide, we lift our prayers up to the Father and find that they are accepted and that we ourselves are received as his adopted sons and daughters. When we gather for Eucharist, we gather in close solidarity with Jesus, our brother. The bond we share with him enables us to relate to God in an entirely different way. During this celebration, our prayers are his prayers; our actions, his actions. We relate to God through Christ, with Christ, and in Christ. He mediates God's love for us and our love for God. He does this because he is one with God and one with us. The Eucharist is a great prayer of thanksgiving. It

celebrates the redeeming love of Christ manifest in the paschal mystery and thanks God for giving us a chance to share in that love and offer it to others.

Concluding Remarks

What can we say by way of conclusion? The Eucharist is a prophetic action of Christ that effects what it symbolizes. It mediates Christ's paschal mystery to the believing community and enables us to worship the Father in Spirit and in truth. It looks to the historical roots of Christ's Easter Pasch, celebrates its presence in Christ's body, the church, and looks to its consummation at the end of time. The Eucharist gives us a foretaste of the heavenly banquet. It gives us Jesus' body and blood as a sign of his ongoing presence in our midst and as food for our pilgrimage through life. It also immerses us in Christ's sacrificial death, an action of selfless love that leads to the empty tomb and his glorious return to the Father.

The Eucharist is Christ's Easter Pasch; as members of his body, it is also our own. It is the ordinary means given us by God to participate in the redemptive action of Christ. Through the Eucharist, Christ acts in and through the members of his body. When we gather for Eucharist, Christ acts as our mediator, uniting our prayers to his and offering them to the Father on our behalf. Through the Eucharist, Christ gives us a share in his resurrection, the new life won for us by his overcoming the forces of sin and death. We experience this new life through the gift of the Spirit who yearns within our hearts and intercedes for us on our behalf with inexpressible groans and longings (cf. Rom 8:26). This Spirit, who prays within us and through us, is the Spirit of Christ our redeemer and mediator before God. When we gather for Eucharist, we celebrate the life in the Spirit made possible for us by Christ's redeeming love. Christ's paschal mystery enables us to participate in the life of the Spirit. That life binds us closely to Christ and the Father and inspires us to create similar bonds with others for the sake of the kingdom.

In this chapter, we have looked at the close relationship between the Eucharist and Christ's paschal mystery. We have seen the importance of looking at the Eucharist as an integrated, dramatic action, with each part of the Mass manifesting an important facet of the meaning of Christ's paschal mystery for our lives. We have examined the various parts of the Mass and have discovered the depths of prayer to which they can lead us. We have also seen the intimate relation that our celebration of the Eucharist has with the rest of life and how our deeper awareness of what takes place during that celebration can help us to respond to the call to Christian discipleship with more dedicated commitment to a life of humble service.

The Eucharist provides us with food for our journey. This food confirms us in our call to discipleship and encourages us to follow the promptings of the Spirit that guide us along the way of conversion. It does so by strengthening the bonds between Christ and the members of his body and by gradually transforming us into the fullness of God's vision for us. The end of the Eucharist and Christ's paschal mystery is to empower us to continue a journey that will ultimately lead us to see God face to face. Hope in the *visio Dei* (beatific vision) permeates every aspect of the Christian spiritual moral life both as an end of our actions and as a fundamental means of achieving our human destiny. Because of its connection with the paschal mystery, the Eucharist keeps this vision before our eyes and helps us to journey toward it.

CHAPTER THREE

The Eucharist as Source for Moral Formation

The new sacrifice of Christians, their spiritual cult, is the *caritas* that comes from the sacrifice of Christ with whom we communicate in the Eucharist. The connection between eucharistic sacrifice and ethics allows the cross to be the unsurpassable form of the Christian's ethical life....The action of the cross of Christ becomes the fundamental action of Christian liturgy and of ethics. The Lord's hands on the cross are simultaneously raised to the Father and extended toward neighbor, and the two directions make one.

Livio Melina
Sharing in Christ's Virtues[1]

We have just seen how the most central of all Christian truths, the paschal mystery, reaches us through the eucharistic liturgy. As offered in the midst of daily parish worship, this mystery should also have something to say about the foundation of our moral lives in Christ. In this chapter, we will examine how the paschal mystery in its sacramental expression offers concrete direction for Catholic moral living. Using again the main sections of the Mass for our basic format, we will outline the interpenetration of a call from God to moral conversion with the eucharistic liturgy and uncover the specifically moral relevance of the paschal mystery. We saw in the first chapter that the paschal mystery is about God's plan to save us from sin and death. Now we will see that, by entering regularly into the mystery of the Eucharist, we progressively become free from enslavement to sin and fear of death, and emerge over time as persons inhabited by the mind of Christ. *This is the most vital of all moral elements: moral conversion.* We will now look at how the liturgy effects such a conversion.

The Penitential Rite: A Call from Sin to Fidelity

We cannot get close to the holy without first turning from evil. This truth is acknowledged within each Mass in the Penitential Rite, as we reviewed in chapter 2. This consciousness of sin is not intended to become a source of self-doubt or hate, because we acknowledge in the context of Christ's prayer to the Father that Christ wants only to communicate divine life to us, not condemnation (e.g., the story of the woman caught in adultery [John 8:11]). The moral conversion to which the Eucharist summons us enables a faithful living out of our human identity. At the very beginning of Catholic worship, in the penitential rite, is *a lesson in Christian anthropology*: we are made for greater things than vice can imagine or even comprehend. We must go forward through the pain of the Penitential Rite, face our infidelities to God, truth, neighbor, and self, and entrust this act of painful self-awareness to the mercy of God. Having done this, our vision begins to clear and we come to reject Satan and his lies (Baptismal Rite) and to welcome the Christ who brings "light to those in darkness" (Penitential Rite, Option 5).

This is a developmental process in cooperation with grace, that is, in cooperation with the Holy Spirit living within us. Participating in one eucharistic liturgy does not normally effect a complete moral conversion for any of us, but the Mass does hold the key to a patient, gentle, yet firm commitment to yield sin over to the healing power of Christ. In the Penitential Rite the church recalls in all its prayers that we need to "prepare" to enter the mysteries of Christ. We enter only as invited guests. We do not take the Eucharist as our own; it is holy, and we are only *in via*, on the way. The church prays before the reception of the Eucharist,

"Lord, I am not worthy to receive you,
but only say the word and I shall be healed."

There is no going into the mystical life, the life of faith, hope, and love as known in the sacraments, except through the crucifixion of sin. The paschal mystery as encountered in the eucharistic liturgy is a knowledge, gained through ritual experience, of the divine plan of salvation that can only first be entered by way of a solid Christian anthropology: we are created in the image of God, and yet we do not bear God's likeness in consistent form. The worship of God through the Christic mysteries and the will's desire to turn from vice create the perfect matrix for giving birth to such a longed-for consistency. To be "like" God is to be a person who loves, that is, who consistently wills the good. From almost the very beginning of the Mass the church is called to take on this challenge as both a means and goal of divine worship. Living the virtuous life as *means* allows the believer to know the deepest possible communion with God. Living the virtuous life as *goal* allows the believer to revel fully in the sharing of divine happiness. Both as means and goal, the virtuous life intersects and is completed by the divine life shared through the paschal mystery. Thus, to become both good and holy, to live a faithful human life as one who is created in the image (our dignity coming from God) and likeness (virtues that prepare and deepen communion with God) of God, one must participate in the eucharistic mystery.

A core action of moral conversion in the eucharistic liturgy is the *Confiteor* or, when this is not prayed, the *Kyrie* alone. As we asserted in chapter 2, one cannot view a single part of the Mass in isolation from others—it is all "Christ's prayer." We are right, however, to emphasize the Penitential Rite in light of its clear moral content. Building upon this would be the Liturgy of the Word and its moral teachings, along with the homily, Eucharistic Prayer, and the actual reception of communion. All of these have the capacity to turn one's mind and will from vice and toward virtue. Beyond these four areas of the Mass we also note the Concluding Rite, as we leave the Mass with our thoughts on those we have been called to serve. In this, we are reminded that moral conversion is solidified within one's heart after repeated efforts actually to practice the many moral virtues. The virtue of worship itself is a practice that over time yields a deeper awareness of the presence of God in others. We are to live our moral lives from the inside out. The virtue of worship makes us vulnerable to the grace of being convicted of our personal sins, and it clearly imparts the graces necessary to resolve to change, but the grace found in actually loving the enemy, overcoming lust, controlling gluttony, or tempering envy roots any virtue within the marrow of our desires. This is not to deny that one can be healed of sinful desires at the Mass, but the normal route for moral conversion appears to be in the work of *willing and desiring,* albeit the work of a will open to the grace of the paschal mystery. As the Mass cannot be strictly compartmentalized without reducing its power as the one "prayer of Christ," so our lives cannot be separated into worship and living the practice of the virtues. These two so constitute the core of the baptized life that we can only know one or the other fully in the interpenetration of both. It was to the *mysterious moral life* that Christ called us when he called us to life and life to the full.

Furthermore, the *Confiteor* prayer is familiar to all Catholics as the one that begins, "I confess to almighty God, and to you my brothers and sisters, that I have sinned through my own fault in my thoughts and in my words, in what I have done, and in what I have failed to do." Let us pause there and see what profound resonance these words have within the truth of moral conversion. First, it does appear slightly jarring that a communal prayer begins with the singular "I," but this is not an attempt to underscore private devotion within a communal prayer. Those who advocate that the church should change the wording to "we" miss a vital anthropological point: *in our sins we all go alone before God.* We all must be confronted by truth, or judged, as individuals. This would be in contrast with the Nicene Creed, which begins, "We believe in one God, the Father, the Almighty...." In this prayer the entire community responds as a body to the collective call of God to be God's people and to respond to this call to faith as one. Sin separates and divides the body of Christ; faith, hope, and love unite it. It is *my* sin that injures the life of the church. Even social sin begins with one person cooperating with an evil that may already be present, through the past cooperation of other individuals, and that now remains caught in the social structures and habits of a community. This is why prophetic action can break the chains of social injustice. Even though its origins and sustenance are somewhat unconscious ("this is the way we have always done things here"—e.g., racist employment policies, sexism, killing of the unborn, cohabitation of unwed couples, and so on), its eradication can begin with the courage and love of truth found in one person. Thus, when we are dealing with sin, we begin with "I confess...."

Second, in this prayer of confession we are immediately exposed to some compelling truths of the moral life. We are addressing God. All sin is an offense to God. Sins are those dispositions leading to action that invert God's loving plan for the human to cherish the other and treat the neighbor as they themselves would like to be treated. It is a fierce and dramatic "no" to the revelation that all men and women are created in God's image. Sinners see only themselves. They admit nothing of the dignity of the other when their self-interest is in jeopardy, and so through pride, anger, lust, envy, greed, gluttony, or a host of other sins, one chooses the self over the welfare of another. The sinner literally chooses not to *see* the worth of one's neighbor. In this we offend God, and we need to address our repentance directly to God, who is the almighty Creator and sustainer of all life. The eucharistic liturgy reveals an anthropology that directly announces that all of us fall short of the glory of God in how we treat God's own beloved creatures and therefore our brothers and sisters. Thus, the *Confiteor* continues by saying that we also confess to one another. The Penitential Rite reminds us that we are entering the holy, that is, communion with the living God in Christ, and so we cannot go further with our worship if we "have something against our brother." The right relationships of Christian living demand that persons be in union with God, with others, and with self. Here the entire direction of Catholic moral life is encapsulated: I cannot enter eternal life if I do not start living its essence of communion with God and others *today*. Now is the time of salvation. Now is the acceptable time.

The prayer also starkly announces that "I have sinned through my own fault." This is both a startling and a refreshing admission in today's Western society in which behaviorist theories of environmental, genetic, and psychological determinism have made their presence felt. In the area of moral choice, the church still teaches that personal freedom is possible. We would say that it is not only *possible* but the linchpin to all moral meaning. Without the reality of human freedom, the power to live in virtue and direct one's life toward the good, there would be little or no meaning to life. We would be literally *determined*. While the church has not accepted theories of determination, it has welcomed the evidence from scientific fields that indicate that genetic makeup, environment (e.g., families of origin, economic conditions, cultural diversity), and psychological factors (unconscious or suppressed truths) *do influence* our behaviors. Therefore, confessors and spiritual directors need to take these powerful waves of influence into consideration when sharing counsel on moral truth, responsibility, and culpability.

The sin confessed in the *Confiteor* is understood not simply as external behavior but includes thoughts and omissions, as well. To modern ears, "in my thoughts and in my words, in what I have done and what I have failed to do" may sound almost neurotic in its level of specificity, but, in fact, saying these words indicates that a person is heading in the direction of mental health and away from pathology. Continuing the reorientation of the person toward fidelity to the human identity, the Penitential Rite reaches a climax in identifying that all conversion from vice passes through the faith-imbued reason that is judging truth and falsity, fidelity and infidelity. The church believes and assures its members that one can reach surety about acts, thoughts, and omissions that are misaligned with the goals of discipleship. In fact, the saints testify to the fact that the closer one moves toward and participates in the paschal mystery, the clearer the mind becomes regarding sin. The knowledge of sin is not intended to be a crushing burden that weighs heavily upon the individual; rather, for those growing in holiness, the knowledge of immoral acts, omissions, and thoughts is seen to be a great gift from the providence of God. Without such knowledge we would never be led to repentance, and hence we would lose our ultimate goal of communion with all that is holy. This section of the Penitential Rite is seen by those desiring moral rectitude as a great grace, completed either by the reception of holy communion or, in the case of mortal sin, the celebration of the sacrament of reconciliation outside of the Mass.

The knowledge of our own personal sins is crucial for coming to real participation in the paschal mystery. This knowledge can be given to us by a searching inventory of our conscience during Mass, or during spiritual reading, or most often by the remarks of those we live with in religious community, family, or parish. No matter the conveyance of truth about our state before God, it is the disposition with which we receive such truth that is crucial. One of the graces of participating in the eucharistic liturgy is a deepening capacity to host the truth about ourselves. It is the goal of the Christian seeking holiness to welcome and even solicit feedback about how one is living life among others. When the truth about our present vices comes to be known by us, how do we host this information? Are we defensive and angry, or do we receive it with humility and ultimately gratitude? With any moral conversion it will be necessary to undergo the pain of self-examination. In this way our predecessors in the faith always spoke about an examination of conscience. Here in the Penitential Rite the reality of conscience comes to the fore-front of Catholic moral living.

Without an interior life no believer can make progress in the spiritual/moral life. All persons are called to an interior life; it is not something simply for those so-called introverts who are more easily predisposed to contemplation and meditation. To call for an interior life as a prerequisite to a virtuous life is simply to acknowledge, since the time of one's baptism, the reality of the indwelling Holy Spirit. The call of the eucharistic liturgy to withstand the pain of self-examination is both an invitation to enter into an honest inven-tory of sins, and if one is unwilling to do that at the present moment, an invitation to pray for the courage to do so in the near future. For those who perceive themselves as being unable to go deep within the soul, the assistance of a pastor or other spiritual director becomes almost a necessity if the moral life is to begin in earnest. For those who feel already "at home" within the soul, there needs to be a lively community life so that introversion is checked and the fruit of med-itation and contemplation shows itself to others in the form of virtue.

Once we begin to go within the soul and confront all the "demons" and complexities of interiority, we begin to realize why the church gave us the next lines of the *Confiteor:*

"I ask blessed Mary, ever virgin,
all the angels and saints,
and you, my brothers and sisters,
to pray for me to the Lord our God."

It becomes known very quickly for those who brave the naming of sin that one needs supernatural assistance if the journey from living in vice to living in virtue is to be accomplished. The saints are sum-moned in our prayer because they are experts in this crossing from vice to virtue. They possess a holy empathy toward us. They also stand continually in the presence of God, in a position to call upon God's mercy for those still in the process of conversion upon earth. The naming of the saints in the liturgy, here and specifically in the eucharistic prayers, reminds us that these holy persons are our mod-els of virtue. The life of a saint is a doorway for us to walk through. Once inside the saint's life, grace invites us to consider our own life and how it measures up to the saint's cooperation with Christ's call to discipleship. This "measuring" is not in the form of comparing one's life to the saint's—this could lead to envy or despair—but rather takes the form of inspiration in the same way one looks upon a role model to emulate in sports, profession, or vocation. "I know I am not a sports or business 'star,' but I want to study how they achieved greatness so I can achieve it in my own way and within my own limits, identity, and mission." The school of holiness teaches us to say, "I want to be an original copy of Christ," not a mimic.[2] To be an original copy, one is cognizant of one's uniqueness as a beloved of God, but at the same time one also knows that Christ is the only model of the true human being. In the communion one has with Christ, the paradox of following Christ and one's own unique appropriation of that call becomes clear. There really is only *one* Saint Francis de Sales, for example, but even his unique discipleship is radically dependent upon the *one* Christ. The eucharistic liturgy gives us the saints as sources for moral reflection and grace. They are the holy ones living now in Christ and pouring out loving prayers for our benefit. The saints who are still *in via* are invoked in this section of the *Confiteor* as well.

Those neighbors who sit in the pew to our left and right are also to be petitioned for prayer. Ironically, we may be more aware of praying to the saints in heaven than with those who worship every Sunday by our side, and yet these brothers and sisters are also powerful in enabling our moral conversions. The church, the body of Christ, is the gathering of those who long to be one with Christ in all they do. Each member of the body of Christ has a role in our moral conversion through prayer and/or example. We often are told that sin is all around us in this Western "culture of death," but grace is all around us as well, in the form of our Christian neighbor in the next office, cubicle, or workbench. The church is all around us— more potently so than evil's influence. The eucharistic liturgy is trying to point us toward one another at the conclusion of the *Confiteor*, begging us not to go the way of conversion alone. To travel the road to holiness alone is to invite our own failure at overcoming sin.

Since sin must be offered up to God in order to have it destroyed in the purifying love of divine compassion, believers know that their moral conversion depends upon this act of sacrifice. How is offering our sins to God a sacrifice? We can look at this on two levels: personal and liturgical. Personally, offering sin to God is the essence of cooperating with the divine initiative to offer us a share in God's life. This offering to God also involves our suffering. *To become holy, then, is to suffer the offering of our sins to God.* It is to separate ourselves from the person we had become under sin's influence, and to become instead a person who is open to the renewing power of grace. The separation from our sin is what causes us psychic pain. This is the struggle of good and evil within us. To so struggle is to undergo an agony, a word in the Western pagan epoch originally related to a sacrifice offered to the gods.

Liturgically, only those who do not enter fully into the Penitential Rite, and all that it directs us to in the faithful executions of our daily duties, would think the word *agony* too extreme. The saints regularly witness to this agony as they allow God to replace sin with a share in the divine life. The immoral thoughts, words, omissions, and actions of our choosing all became enmeshed within our character, and to alter that character toward virtue is, indeed, an agony: a painful sacrifice in the service of holiness. To address this reality, the eucharistic liturgy sings out the *Kyrie.* In this ancient plea for mercy, the church understands how the agony of moral conversion can circumvent the good intentions of believers to move toward virtue. In this pleading prayer that closes the Penitential Rite, the church floods the consciousness of worshippers with images of God's mercy and healing power. In a series of statements about our sinful human condition and the nature of God's salvific will, we come to know that, despite our weak attempts to fulfill the call to moral conversion, God will meet us with mercy and compassion. This knowledge helps to temper self-hate or despair in the long journey of relinquishing sin and taking up virtue.

Within the invocation of the *Kyrie* are factual statements about the identity of God in Christ and about Christian anthropology. From this one section of the liturgy alone could be culled many meditations on the fact of sin and the empowering divine response to it in the mystery of the incarnation of the Second Person of the Blessed Trinity. About our human condition we learn: humanity is sinful; we are in need of reconciliation, peace, and healing; we live in darkness and long for the light; we have the destiny of being raised to new life in Christ; we need to be strengthened in order to become holy; we are forgiven our sins by Christ; and it is Christ who nourishes us and feeds us with the Eucharist. About God we learn that God is mercy and love, God heals us, calls us even though we are in sin, gathers us together to bring peace, comes to us in scripture and in the sacraments, possesses might, became human as the Son of Mary, has a mission of reconciliation and intercession for his people, is capable of raising the dead to life in the Spirit, brings light to darkness, forgives sin, and feeds us with his own body and blood. Further, Christ is seen to be the way to the Father, the giver of consoling truth, and the protective good shepherd. Any sound moral theology needs to look at all these human realities and divine mysteries in order to come to a realistic view regarding moral conversion and virtue formation. The relationship between the human person and God's salvific will is the drama of moral conversion and the key to articulating what human happiness is all about. Through the themes of healing, nourishing, raising to new life, light, mercy, forgiveness, peace, reconciliation, and more, the moral theologian can construct a series of meditations on the grace of God, as God wills our well-being and not our destruction. This beneficence, we are told in our worship, is at the very heart of who God is (God is filled with "life and goodness" and holiness [Eucharistic Prayer 1]), and therefore we can trust God to bring us out of the darkness of moral evil and into the light. God is for us. A fitting response after the Penitential Rite is glorious praise (the Gloria). We are compelled to thank such a God, who "takes away the sin of the world" and who "alone...is Holy."

The Penitential Rite is rich with thematic gems to mine in our study of moral theology. In the overarching context of *moral conversion* we come to reflect upon the meaning of *Christian anthropology, sin, virtue,* and *forgiveness.* All of these themes arise organically from the liturgy itself, and they find their perennial nature in the study of moral theology from the deep root they tap within the mystery of the human person before God.

The Liturgy of the Word: Conscience Formation

Next we move to the Liturgy of the Word, the time of rapt listening, of receptive listening, of renewed commitment to take on the "mind of Christ" (1 Cor 2:16). The Liturgy of the Word is the opening of revelation to the gathered assembly. This part of eucharistic worship is as wide and rich and deep as scripture itself. There is no end to the moral wisdom that comes to the listening heart during this time within worship. The moral principles we can draw from the Liturgy of the Word are both universal and personal. God addresses one as a member of a wider church, and yet God is addressing each person through the Holy Spirit in order to uniquely summon that person to conversion from sin.

What moral guidance can we learn from the Liturgy of the Word itself? In entering the Liturgy of the Word we are reminded that God invites us to be active, receptive listeners. The Liturgy of the Word must be placed within the context of the whole worship service—in the matrix of the whole service, the members of the church are called to listen to, hear, and heed the word of God, and then to respond by taking it out into the world, thus embodying moral living in concrete expressions of truth, service, and peace in the course of their daily lives. In this rhythm we see the church sharing in Mary's disposition, "Let it be with me according to your word" (Luke 1:38). The church in the Liturgy of the Word becomes Marian, because we *all* are invited to receive and *do* the Word as Mary did. As we affirmed in chapter 2, the Word of God is always effective, first changing the hearer of the Word, and then changing others as a result of the witness given by those Catholics who immerse themselves in culture through work, politics, art, education, health care, and more. The Liturgy of the Word has the power to change the rapt listener's mind from a tomb to a womb (Raniero Cantalamessa). We are bid to let the Holy Spirit bring what is dead in us to life. In this way we share with Mary in the carrying of Christ into time.

Rapt listening, then, or obedience, is the virtue called for during the Liturgy of the Word. This kind of listening is not a passive obedience but an active dialogue with God in a search for truth. In this listening one is, with God's help, distinguishing the voices of truth from those of deception. Reading or hearing the Word of God is the premier environment for hearing the truth from its source. If this virtue of rapt listening is weak, we are bid to pray for it during the Liturgy of the Word as well. It is not simply *the* virtue for the duration of the Liturgy of the Word, however; it is the virtue for entering the paschal life in itself. Through obedience the worshipper encounters the wonder of Christ's own interior disposition: "My food is to do the will of him who sent me" (John 4:34). As was said in chapter 2, the Liturgy of the Word seeks to help us to open our hearts to God's Word so that it might take root there and be born within us. It affirms our identity as members of Christ's body and readies us for even deeper participation in Christ's paschal mystery.

Within the Liturgy of the Word we also glimpse a vast continuity of doctrinal tradition within our church. Scripture carries the truths by which the church lives and rightly forms a core source of moral formation for its members. It is this doctrinal tradition, coupled with contemporary oral tradition (the homily), that places the worshipper within a context for proper conscience formation. In fact, here within the Liturgy of the Word is conscience formation par excellence. This part of the liturgy is a collective *lectio divina,* filling our minds with grace and calling us to abide in truth. This *lectio* is a prayerful entrance of the mind and heart into the paschal mystery of Christ. It is not necessarily an experiential entrance, however, but simply an openness to be spoken to by God. God cannot speak to us without an affective component—without touching our hearts—but this affective component does not necessarily reach a level of what we commonly call mystical ecstasy. Still, holy listening to the Word is an event that changes the heart and assists in realigning the conscience to adhere to the voice of truth, who is Christ.

In the Liturgy of the Word one encounters Christ, who invites the worshipper to know him better in the contemplation of his life and word through scripture. Contemplation, our loving attention given to the person of God, is the key to the formation of conscience within worship. Without such attention one may simply be showing up for worship but not truly participating in its personal dynamism. Only with such participation can the truth penetrate the conscience. Listening to scripture proclaimed at Mass is rightly described as a mystic listening, because through it the person of faith is invited into the life of God. When the Word is proclaimed and we actively receive it, we are living in the conscious presence of God, constituting a mystic base to our mind's faith formation. When the scriptures of the day entail moral truth, the worshipper encounters the person of Christ as teacher of truth. To this teacher the believer gives obedient love. In this kind of love one is vulnerable and docile, hungry for knowledge of God's will above all things, because like Christ the disciple sees the Father's will as "his [or her] food."

We find then in the Liturgy of the Word a key building block to any moral theology, the activation of an awakened conscience eager to be formed by truth. The content of this formation is specific to the readings of the day and the interpretive homily. This content will be crucial to forming a mind able and eager to judge truth in the light of discipleship. Believers will want to be docile before the Word proclaimed because in it they know their mind will find rest and no longer be buffeted by the waves and winds of "this world" (Rom 12:1–2).

Liturgy of the Eucharist:
Virtue's Origin in Charity Itself

After the penitential prayers and the Liturgy of the Word, the church, following ancient Jewish traditions and the actions of Christ himself, gives us the breaking of the bread. Here, as was reviewed in chapters 1 and 2, we are at the heart of the paschal mystery. From within the sacramental mystery of the Eucharist, God the Father, through Christ and in the Holy Spirit, reaches out to the human race to overturn the horror of death. This resurrection hope is one that is not restricted to physical death alone, but includes the yearning of the human person to overcome sin and enter life—life to the full: holiness (John 10:10). Thus we bring our fears of death to the Liturgy of the Eucharist and beg the Father to take us up into the Christic mystery of crucified self-offering so that we may know newness of life. Here we confront the mystery of being embodied souls. We know that a faithful human life is one that neither denigrates the body, nor exults the spirit in isolation from the body. Rather, we struggle for integration and receive such as a gift from a life of faith, hope, and love. The Liturgy of the Eucharist is the well of such a gift. The more we partake of its contents, the more we find ourselves yielding to the power of divine charity, a charity that raises Christ in his unity as embodied soul. The Eucharist becomes a source of integrated life for us all. It dispenses the grace of resurrection life and thus carries with it the origin of all virtues. How can we understand the Liturgy of the Eucharist, in its symbol of Christ's death and resurrection, to be the origin of all virtue?

Virtue is commonly understood to be embedded dispositions or character traits that ready a person for eager and easy action in favor of what is morally good. The virtuous person loves moral goodness and desires to enact, through free will, only those behaviors that are consonant with the truth about human identity. In developing these enduring character traits, which ready one for action on behalf of moral goodness, the person experiences happiness. This is the true end of virtuous living: knowing the serenity and peace of being lovingly congruent with moral truth. For the Christian, this kind of life has its source in the paschal mystery, because it is Christ himself who is the embodiment of all virtue. It is, therefore, correct to say that for the Christian the goal of moral living is not simply virtue but holiness: morally good behavior enacted in charity and out of the power of Christ, who dwells within us.

The one "who humbled himself to share in our humanity" has become the bread of life and our spiritual drink. In the Liturgy of the Eucharist we come to feed upon virtue itself. Thus in the Communion Rite, which completes the Liturgy of the Eucharist, we actually become one with him who is the only one to have lived a perfect moral life. He gives himself to us not to underscore such a distinction but in order *to share with us* the power and capacity to become good and holy as well. When one is well disposed to receive this communion, it has powerful effects upon satisfying one's desire to become holy. As the Christmas Preface II exclaims,

> "He has come to lift up all things to himself,
> to restore unity to creation,
> and to lead mankind from exile into your heavenly
>   kingdom."

Furthermore, in the Christmas Preface III, we pray,

> "God has become one with man,
> and man has become one again with God."

Christ is the integrative power of reconciliation, leading us from vice to virtue. The Lenten Prefaces also echo the identity of Christ as the one who restores us to virtue and holiness through union with God.

> "You give us a spirit of loving reverence for you, our Father,
> and of willing service to our neighbor.
> As we recall the great events that gave us new life in Christ,
> you bring the image of your Son to perfection within us"
>   (Lent I).

In Lent Preface II we read,

> "You give us strength to purify our hearts,
> to control our desires,
> and so to serve you in freedom.
> You teach us how to live in this passing world
> with our heart set on the world that will never end."

Finally,

> "You ask us to express our thanks by self-denial.
> We are to master our sinfulness and conquer our pride.
> We are to show to those in need your goodness to
>   ourselves" (Lent III).

The entire corpus of Eucharistic Prefaces announces Christ and his paschal mystery as the origin of the power of goodness over evil, light over darkness. It is Christ who restores us to friendship with God. It is he who strengthens us from within and orders us toward the sacred:

> "By his dying he has destroyed our sins.
> By his rising he has raised us up to holiness of life"
>   (Preface for Passion Sunday).

In the Preface for the Feast of Christ the King we are taught that Christ brings us into specific virtues of truth, justice, love, and peace. On the Feast of the Body and Blood of Christ we are reminded that it is Christ who strengthens us and transforms us into his likeness. The Liturgy of the Eucharist leaves no doubt that the paschal mystery has moral and sanctifying ends.

It remains true, however, that each person needs to enflesh this eucharistic mystery and struggle in the spirit to relinquish vice and take up holy living. This enfleshing of the Christian life happens in the nooks and crannies of the ordinariness of our days, and not simply at worship. What is of great significance, however, is that the power to grow in virtuous holiness is now drawn *from within the human soul, a soul inhabited by the paschal mystery*. Since our baptism and within our regular communion with Christ in the Eucharist, we "become less" ("He must increase, but I must decrease" [John 3:30]), and his life living in us becomes dominant. Paradoxically, it is a dominant life that only invites us to service, self-emptying, and obedience to charity and truth. It is, as was reviewed in chapter 1, a life of divinization. Through the liturgy we have access to the paschal mystery, making this sacrament our normal route to moral transformation and healing. Let us look more closely at the Liturgy of the Eucharist to see how it enacts the healing of vice and our moral transformation into persons who take on the virtues of Christ.

The Eucharistic Prayers

Raniero Cantalamessa has noted this about the mystery of the Eucharist: "Our own contribution [to the liturgy] consists only in accepting grace, in not wasting the treasure, in not extinguishing the lamp once lit....In fact, however, in this contribution there is room for the entire moral commitment of the Christian."[3] The acceptance of grace is far from an inert stance. It is in fact the crucial disposition to all things Christian. We know it in our own lives and in the lives of the saints as the power of humility and the activity of an open, searching heart. It is a journey that seeks only to rest in the person of Christ. "We have found the Messiah" (John 1:41). The acceptance of grace is the acceptance of friendship with Christ, and from within this friendship comes a share in all of Christ's virtues.

To accept grace is to enter the Eucharist at its white-hot center, the Eucharistic Prayer. Here we reach the action of Christ that he extends to all his followers, "Follow me" (Luke 5:27). Follow him where? We are bid to follow him into the mystery of his self-offering upon the cross out of obedient love for the Father. Within this portion of the Liturgy of the Eucharist we stand ready to accept the friendship Christ offers to all those who respond to his call: "Whoever does the will of God is my brother and sister and mother" (Mark 3:35), and, "I do not call you servants any longer...but I have called you friends" (John 15:15). There is a real shift in relation to Christ once we come to accept grace and enter the life Christ is living in the presence of his Father for all eternity, a life embodied in his Gethsemane suffering—"...not what I want but what you want" (Matt 26:39). In this life, one is not continually suffering; in fact, once the crucifixion of sin is accomplished, doing the will of the Father is *the* way to happiness. What applicable moral truths flow from this mystery of accepting the grace of Christ's Pasch?

In the first Eucharistic Prayer we note its focus upon the Father, and Christ's self-offering to him. We are immersed in petitionary prayers for the living and the dead, and we are covered with the coming of the Holy Spirit upon the bread and wine, and our own gift of self as well. In the closing lines of this prayer we read,

> "Through [Christ our Lord] you give us all these gifts.
> You fill them with life and goodness,
> you bless them and make them holy."

Just before this the priest prays that the gathered assembly may come to share in "the fellowship" of the apostles, martyrs, and saints. Here is the core of our transformation within the Mass. We are asking God to continually have our hearts and character reshaped by grace so that we might become fit for heaven. We are, in other words, begging for the infused virtues, which dispose us to receive grace upon grace. To reach this end is to live a life repulsed by immorality and serenely content to know only Christ and him crucified. In the center of the Eucharistic Prayer is Christ's action of obedient love upon the cross and his resurrection power; at its margins are the humble pleadings of his followers for some share in that resurrection power. To receive such power is be engraced for a life of virtue.

This aspect of the Eucharistic Prayer becomes even more explicit in the following verse from the Preface of Eucharistic Prayer II:

> "For our sake he opened his arms on the cross;
> he put an end to death
> and revealed the resurrection.
> In this he fulfilled your will
> and won for you a holy people."

It becomes clear that this act of Christ's is for us and for our holiness. The act that opened such a possibility is Christ's and Christ's alone, but because it was "for our sake," we can become a "holy people." A further reference to the transforming power of the Eucharist is given in the close of the third Eucharistic Prayer,

> "We hope to enjoy for ever the vision of your glory,
> through Christ our Lord, from whom all good things come."

Christ is the author of goodness, and the one to transform us and conform us inwardly to virtue by the power of his Holy Spirit. Further on, in Eucharistic Prayer IV, we see explicitly that the Holy Spirit guides our moral renewal:

"And that we might live no longer for ourselves but for him
     [Christ],
he sent the Holy Spirit from you, Father,
as his first gift to those who believe,
to complete his work on earth
and bring us the fullness of grace."

To come to accept grace, the very life of God living within us, is the linchpin for personal moral transformation. It is literally living out of the power of the resurrection: the end to death and dead things, sin, and the beginning of life on high in Jesus Christ. Following John 6, Dom Columba Marmion concludes that the Eucharist is the bread of life because "it places in our very bodies the germ of the resurrection."[4] It is the Eucharist that "excites charity and sustains fervor," rendering the soul "prompt and devoted in God's service." Marmion summarizes his point in this way: "Christ, ever living, acts in silence, but sovereignly in the innermost depths of the soul in order to transform it into Himself; that is the most precious effect of this heavenly food; he that eateth of my flesh and drinketh my blood abideth in Me and I in him."[5]

Brian Johnstone has also noted the importance of the resurrection in developing ideas on the moral life. "The moral life can be best understood as a resurrection of the soul....The divine power that drives this life is the very power that raises Jesus from the dead. The transformations...in which we move out of the death of sin into the newness of life are realizations in our own history of the divine power that raised Jesus."[6] Johnstone argues that our very desire to leave sin behind and take up virtue is a thirst for the resurrection.

Saint Thomas Aquinas argues that the resurrection was necessary to inform the life of the faithful. "This word 'inform' does not mean merely to give information, but to form in the sense of constituting its nature, purpose and meaning. In the same way we say that charity informs all the other virtues....St. Thomas is saying that our moral life is formed not by love in general...but by divine love precisely as the power that raised Jesus from the dead."[7] The mystery of the resurrection should be central to the moral life. If this is true, then the Eucharist, wherein the paschal mystery is laid before us, should be the chief place of moral transformation. When is the last time the liturgy converted us from sin?

The Communion Rite:
Internalizing the Transforming Power of Grace

In the Communion Rite we come upon an encapsulation of all that went before. We are reminded in the Lord's Prayer how we need to turn to the Father for forgiveness of sins. He is the one who "delivers us from evil and grants us peace." Throughout the Communion Rite we are once again immersed in our need for forgiveness and reconciliation with God and others. It is the theme of the Penitential Rite revisited. This revisiting is underscored in the Lamb of God prayer said during the breaking of the bread, where we beg Christ to have mercy on us, to take away our sins, and then to grant us peace. The prayer with the most powerful moral theme within it, however, is one said silently by the priest just before he elevates the host along with the words,

> "This is the Lamb of God
> who takes away the sins of the world.
> Happy are those who are called to his supper."

The private prayer of the priest is, "Lord Jesus Christ, Son of the living God, by the will of the Father and the work of the Holy Spirit your death brought life to the world. By your holy body and blood free me from all my sins, and from every evil. Keep me faithful to your teaching, and never let me be parted from you." In this prayer the entire paschal mystery is summarized within the context of conversion from sin and the power of God to protect us from further sin. Special emphasis is placed upon the power of God in the Eucharist to keep the priest faithful to the teachings of Christ. Thus we see here the power of the paschal mystery carried within the Mass to initiate, sustain, and empower from within fidelity to Christ, who is the truth. With this the priest and congregation are readied to receive the living God under sacramental signs. After this reception the only thing left to do is be silent, and then go to love and serve the Lord and one another. Out of the silence of communion, we hear the call to live the moral life within culture, and we go forth from worship to do the truth.

Observations

In reviewing the eucharistic liturgy within the framework of the paschal mystery we have uncovered several key points relevant to the Catholic moral life:

1. *Worship calls us to moral conversion.* As was noted in chapter 1, we come in contact with the paschal mystery first and foremost through our participation in the eucharistic liturgy. The liturgy conforms us to Christ in his virtues and allows God to work in human lives through our powers of intellect, will, and affection, and in ways even beyond our conscious awareness. Since all this is true, our worship becomes the site of our own moral conversion, and it provides affective and intellectual content for moral reflection. The fullness of our human powers is addressed in worship, and therefore we can respond in full to the truth of Christ's paschal mystery. Since we encounter this mystery at each Mass, we would do well to approach it with expectations of healing of sin, transformation of ideas, and a deepening of our love for God and the moral good. For our worship to be a powerhouse of healing, it helps to see it as such and appropriately petition God for the specific healing we need in the area of vice. The liturgy is the action of Christ that invites us to join him in saying, "Father, into your hands I commend my spirit" (Luke 23:46). In so doing we align our lives to the obedient love of Christ; from such a love all power to lead morally good lives is given to us. So much power is granted, in fact, that soon we transcend the language of "morally good lives" and begin to understand this reality as holiness and sanctity: *finitum capax infinitum,* the finite is capable of containing the infinite. When we do not cooperate with the call to virtue and instead choose sin, this same loving power calls us back to God through the sacrament of reconciliation. So, we might suffer our conversions, but in the truth of the paschal mystery we never despair of our own weaknesses.

2. *Worship helps us identify an authentic Christian anthropology.* Human beings are simply complex. We are both simple in our identity as the *imago Dei* and complex as those who desire wrongly and

therefore act viciously. Once we lose the truth of who we are, it becomes that much more difficult to know the peace of happiness. We are "loved-nothings": if God did not love us we would not exist. All depends upon our participating in this truth. It is worship that keeps this truth in balance. Living out of the Spirit, we can live in the tension of knowing we are loved but knowing also that this love is an undeserved gift. At times we do not live within this tension gracefully and believe that we are either simply "loved," which leads to pride, or simply "nothing," which leads to despair. To choose such extremes is the personal origin of all our sins. The last sin we committed was because we thought we were "everything," pride, or because we thought we were "nothing," self-hate, despair. Worship acts against this fractured view of the human person and keeps the truth alive within us. We are the beloved of God who need healing and transformation, and without such we perish. Since the liturgy is a source of healing and transformation, in that it is our entryway into the paschal mystery, we approach with humility and gratitude. These virtues then become the proper disposition of the person who knows Christ—not pride or despair, but humility and gratitude. Out of these virtues will flow a life of moral rectitude and wisdom. In staying close to the mystery of Christ in public worship, we stay close to the truth of who we are as human beings, because it is Christ who fully reveals humanity to itself.[8]

3. *Worship heals us of sin and strengthens us to fight against temptation.* Sin is always met with the forgiveness of Christ for those disposed to receive it. If we begin to believe and then act out of the erroneous notion that we are everything or we are nothing, what awaits us in Christ is compassion, mercy, and forgiveness, not condemnation. This is good news, indeed. The less than good news is that to get to the point of receiving divine mercy, we must suffer our own conversion from sin. There is in each conversion a share in the agony Christ experienced in the Garden of Olives. We are to struggle with the evil that has become a part of us, that has formed our character and bent and broken us. Now, through the grace we experience in worship, we enter a struggle to go toward light and healing, even as evil's deceptions continue to attract us in a mighty way. We can, like Christ in his agony, feel like throwing ourselves to the ground and pleading with the Father to "let this cup pass by" (Luke 22:42). It will not pass by, however, for those who are serious about holi-

ness. The passing over from sin to virtue is an inescapable agony for those who have entertained evil down to their bones. Any healing the paschal mystery offers is a healing that fills us only after we have borne the pain of facing the truth about ourselves. We tend not to live in humility and gratitude as "loved-nothings" but instead tend to take to ourselves all power; or despairing, we sin against the Holy Spirit and seek no refuge in the compassion of God, believing God held none for us. Once this dark night is negotiated in prayer, tears, and counsel, however, then the healing rays of Christ's resurrected light appear as invitation and not threat. We become eager to be in his presence at worship so as to seek out further healing and strength and avoid slipping again into pride or despair. Worship teaches us and enacts the reality that holiness is ours, but first we must pass through the crucible of the penitential life: the confrontation with the truth about what sin has done to us.

4. *Worship highlights the need to develop an interior life and correctly form the conscience out of loving obedience.* In order to sustain any moral conversion, we need to develop a lively interior life. We need to get comfortable going within our souls in order to listen to Christ's voice direct our every action in accord with his truth and life. The pastoral task of helping people discern the voices within their souls is crucial to helping believers reach their end as those who participate in the life of God. In the eucharistic liturgy we have a rich environment within which to practice the presence of God. Through a combination of prayers, scripture readings, symbolic actions, and silence, worshippers, over many years, can gain a certain level of control over their thoughts. In knowing Christ, one is not subject to the passing age but is obliged to listen only to the Master's voice. The interior life becomes simple as our spiritual lives progress in earnest. As one yields more and more to grace, one notices how the mind is reaching now for only one thing: the truth. Whereas before one unthinkingly chose vice, or worse, knowingly rejected truth and chose immorality, now the one who welcomes the paschal mystery can only stand for virtuous choices, beginning to think more like God, who hates sin. A conscience that is formed by the paschal mystery will be one that adheres to a life of loving obedience. This stance of loving obedience will define seekers of truth and color their interior life with only shades of Christ's own longings. With each communion, with each eager listening to the Word of God, with each

year of "going in peace to love and serve the Lord and one another," one will take on the "mind of Christ" (1 Cor 2:16).

5. *Worship underscores the lives of saints as sources of moral reflection and grace.* In order to be graced with the mind of Christ, we need the example and graces of those who have gone before us to heaven and those who are already beginning their heaven beside us as neighbors and brothers and sisters in Christ. The eucharistic liturgy highlights the life, power, and abiding relevance of saints as it runs its course throughout the liturgical year. Some examples of how it does so were given above. Beyond this we cannot fail to mention our frequent encounter with the saints in the liturgy through its feasts and memorials. If the homilist so chose, the congregation could hear about saints' lives or teachings on an almost daily basis. In our worship, we are flooded with reverence for the lives of those who cooperated with grace, went through the suffering of their own moral conversions, and ended their days in the grace of paschal living. Over the last forty years or so there has been a waning of interest in the lives of the saints due to, in some cases, poorly written biographies and/or translations of their works. This has changed recently, and now the saints are prominent again in scholarship, high quality popular publishing, and personal piety. This latest resurgence of interest in the lives of the saints can only deepen our respect for the liturgy as an ecclesial environment that never removed them from prominence.

Since the saints are alive, they intercede for us at our worship. Beyond this powerful relationship they have with the church militant, their writings and biographies serve us further as sources of moral reflection and inspiration. It is good to search for favorite saints, blessed ones that resonate with our own struggles against vice or share our particular vocation or professional interests. The generosity of God's grace is seen in the number and variety of saints given to the church. Pondering their lives in prayer and study and emulating them in virtue should become a prime source of moral conversion and reflection. These sources are, at times, more satisfactory in moving the soul to conversion than the many theoretical books on moral theology that have a more limited and academic focus. It is especially exemplary to attend the masses of your favorite saints and plead their intercession on their feast days.

6. *Worship enables us to share in the divine life, making growth in virtue a work of the indwelling mystery of Christ and not simply our*

own willing of the moral good. Perhaps this aspect of our observations is the most crucial, for here we are really pondering the fruit of the paschal mystery. The moral life is popularly seen at times to be a bore, a lot of work, a struggle. It is imagined to be a "school day or work day" and not a "weekend." There is, of course, work in the moral life, but after passing over the work of grave attachments to vice, the work of moral conversion can actually become fascinating and energizing because we come to realize that it is God's life being lived in us for our benefit, for our happiness. The moral life is one of faith, hope, and love. It is at its depth the unfolding of one's friendship with Christ. As a seed, this kind of living began at baptism and began to bloom in grace according to God's timetable and our own developmental capacities. In the prime of moral living we actually seek mortifications and service to others as a way of life. God's life in us makes our own choosings burdensome. The saints begin to yield the will over to God more and more each day, and become less trusting of their own wits and will. "Do you not realize that Jesus Christ is in you?" (2 Cor 13:5). We are called to let Christ reign in our hearts, and in so doing our taste for holiness grows and our distaste for vice increases in proportion. At the Eucharist, our deepening life, based in our centered hearts, reveals that communion becomes the very lifeblood of our day, for without the deepening of God's life in us, we come to wither before the temptations of vice. Only in drawing from the indwelling divine life, which we receive substantially at the Eucharist, is the moral life fully and finally a light burden.

7. *Worship unleashes the power of grace and enables our acceptance of it so that we may no longer live for ourselves but for the good of others. The acceptance of grace is the acceptance of friendship with Christ, and to accept his friendship is to share in his virtues.* To draw life from the Eucharist is to become a man or woman for others. We only become centered on promoting the moral good of others when we are centered upon Christ within ourselves. The simplistic battle between the interior life and the active life is revealed in a truly eucharistic ethic. One cannot withstand the many needs of the poor and needy without drawing from an interior life of prayer and communion with the indwelling God. Without such spiritual strength, serving the good of others draws resentment from us, not good works. Union with Christ, who dwells within our consciences, gives us the strength to withstand and support the moral conver-

sion of others. It also guides our own moral conversion so that as far as possible our spiritual poverty and weakness do not become an oppressive burden upon others as well. To live out of our interior friendship with Christ is to live in a state of shared virtue with him. Over time we become like him whom we love. This is the way of holiness. The more we open ourselves to his real presence abiding within us and in his church, the more we will notice his character traits becoming our own. Generally, we will notice our lack of interest in pleasing our selfish nature. More specifically, we will notice that the vices we practiced, once sweet, now seem bitter. A moral conversion drawn from a eucharistic life is one that renders the believer both progressively spiritual and concerned with the moral and temporal good of others. It is the source of a complete Christian ethic.

Concluding Remarks

The eucharistic liturgy stands as a powerful source for both moral formation and conversion. In the Catholic ethos, the liturgy holds the central place in conscience formation, because within its dual movements of Liturgy of the Word and Liturgy of the Eucharist is contained the crux of the paschal mystery. This is not to say that automatic answers to moral questions will always be delivered at the Mass for inquiring Catholics. What it does mean is that any answer discerned as a result of counsel or spiritual direction must coalesce with the Christic action of the liturgy. Only in this way can the actions of each person's life be conformed to this same action, so much so as to participate in it. By its very nature sin cannot enter the paschal mystery. It is the mission of pastoral leadership to lead parishioners into a life of moral mystery—one wherein our freedom and our virtues have their source in the paschal mystery as enfleshed in the liturgy, so that our public Catholic lives embody that same Christic self-offering.

CHAPTER FOUR

The Three Ways, Liturgy, and Moral Living

The grace that restores us, that purifies us, does so only through raising us to a participation in the divine life, a participation which cannot be conceived apart from the living presence of God within us, a presence which, by its sole and proper power, makes us live in union with Him.

Louis Bouyer,
Introduction to Spirituality[1]

In this chapter we will describe how an individual's and a community's spiritual/moral formation (i.e., conscience and virtue formation) flows from a faith-filled participation in the paschal mystery as expressed in the ongoing process of purgation-illumination-union within the Eucharist. It is there where we access the paschal mystery, establishing it as the foundational and underlying pattern that guides moral conversion and informs the daily lives of Christians. Here, then, we continue with a eucharistic approach to formation but emphasize in a much more concrete manner, through the traditional three ways of spiritual progress (purgative, illuminative, and unitive), what this means specifically for daily Christian living.

What Are the Three Ways?

One of the clearest renderings of the three ways comes from the thirteenth-century Carthusian monk Hugh of Balma. The first way of spiritual progress is one of cleansing or purification. In it the Christian is "disposed for learning true wisdom." The second way of spiritual progress is illumination. Here the believer's searching for wisdom is met and completed by love. Finally, there is the unitive way, "in which the spirit carried aloft by *God alone* [emphasis added] is led beyond every reason."[2] Another more contemporary approach to the three ways comes from Louis Bouyer in his *Introduction to Spirituality*.[3] Bouyer cautions us not to look at the three ways in any determined fashion. We are to see them more or less as "predominant aspects" along the journey to holiness, not as "successive forms," as if purification is strictly followed by illumination that in turn determines union.[4] For Bouyer the purgative way is a period of struggle against habitual sin and vice. The way of illumination has taken some hold on the believer when the struggle against sin is outweighed by the practice of virtue. In this aspect of spiritual living, the gravity of sensual temptation lessens and the person begins to be intrigued by the spiritual and intellectual truths of following Christ. The believer sets out on a course of meditation on the Word of God, attending to the Word and having the mind and affections formed by the Word. The Christian, says Bouyer, is given a "new conscience."[5] This kind of conscience works in such a way that charity founds and moves the person to obey the truth conscience comes to recognize. The unitive way, finally, is the phase in which we live out of the gifts of the Holy Spirit. Again, we emphasize with Bouyer that these are not strictly successive phases. One can possess virtue even while struggling with sin; in fact, it is necessary to have some virtue in order to enter the struggle.[6] A person on the way to holiness is indeed on the way, and not in any manner living a perfect life. We all approach the call of Christ to come and follow him from within an environment of "weeds and wheat" (Matt 13:24ff).

Purgation and Illumination

All moral conversion from the beginning is the work of grace. God is not going to "substitute" himself for our own human nature; God is, instead, working to "regenerate" our nature.[7] We will deal with both the purgative way and the illuminative together, since their modes of operation interpenetrate one another. Overall, the first two ways help one develop a taste for the things of God. Purgation and illumination are a progressive letting go of vice and taking up of divine things: scripture, prayer, fasting, good works, and worship. In this way we look forward to the day when we will be ruled not by sin but by the indwelling Spirit and so come to possess a disposition of holy indifference. This indifference is not some kind of withdrawal of compassion for others or the self, but a simple centeredness in God that will not allow anything other than God to usurp God's place. As this taste for the things of God deepens in the Christian, there comes to birth a simple life, one that is built within the first two ways by our free choices and God's grace.

In the early stages of purification and illumination, we need a guide into the soul, a guide who will be able to teach us the ways of obedience. According to these ways, we are purified of sin and reoriented to the first stages of virtue by attending to the Word of God in love. A spiritual guide will also help interpret the Word, as will other sources such as the *Catechism* and worship itself. A spiritual guide will help us to examine our conscience, but not to the detriment of or as a replacement for prayer. The ways of both purification and illumination facilitate making room for Christ; they don't end in us becoming lodged in ourselves through introspection.[8]

The hallmark of illumination is the engraced work of *taking up virtue,* as a completion of the hallmark of purification, which is the *letting go of vice.* This complementary dynamic continues well into the Christian's mature years, even extending, for smaller sins, until death. To be illumined is to be filled with charity so that one has achieved a self-mastery. It is here that we can speak of the biblical virtue of meekness.[9] "The earth which [the meek] will inherit...is obviously the kingdom of heaven....But I believe it also includes the peaceful possession of ourselves...which is the prerogative of those who have driven from their souls and their lives the tumult of violence and division sown by sin."[10]

The dynamic of entering purification and illumination happens in the context of a Christian's daily duties. The painful aspect of purification is its relevance to acts of immorality present in the normal course of each day. We are to be purified not of some *abstract* pride, but from "my inability ever to ask for forgiveness from my children," for example. We are to be purified not from some generalized notion of gluttony, but from "my habit of taking food first over the needs of my spouse or children, as well as thinking that my quantity of food is subjectively determined by my appetite." We are purified not from some theoretical idea of lust, but from "my desire to wander through internet pornography at will." We are purified not from some abstract sense of anger, but from "my lack of self-control when employees do not immediately follow orders, or correctly succeed in a project according to my commands." The concrete and personal reality of being purified truly makes this aspect of the moral/spiritual life a crucifixion. It is the necessary embracing of personal pain that makes moral conversion a reality from which many run. In the end, *ideas* about being good are embraced enthusiastically by Christians, but *actually enacting* the truth of these ideas is somewhat less enthusiastically enfleshed. This is not surprising since Jesus taught us that his way was "narrow" (Luke 13:24).

The way of illumination comes to our aid, however, and gives us hope that this narrow passage can be successfully negotiated. To be illumined is to be taught the way of the Lord (Ps 25:4). As John Paul II has written,

> To imitate and live out the love of Christ is not possible for man by his own strength alone. He becomes capable of this love only by virtue of a gift received....Only in the mystery of Christ's redemption do we discover the concrete possibilities of man. It would be a very serious error to conclude that the church's teaching is essentially only an ideal which must be adapted...to the so-called concrete possibilities of man....But what are the concrete possibilities of man? And of which man are we speaking? Of man dominated by [sin] or of man redeemed by Christ? And if redeemed man still sins, this is not due to an imperfection of Christ's redemptive act, but to man's will not to avail himself of the grace which flows from that act.[11]

There is much hope in the illuminative process. The Christian stands closer to the sources of moral formation and draws from their wisdom and purposes as conveyors of grace. Therefore, in this stage of conversion we seek out holy people to converse with and observe; read the scriptures, lives of the saints, and devotional and spiritual books; practice new ways of responding to the needs of others; and revel in the fact that we are actually seeing the needs of others and not simply our own. There is real hope here, but the Christian knows that it is hope in God, in God's promises to be with us always and to give us his very life. We share in this life by receiving the Holy Spirit and communing with this Spirit in all our prayers about moving from vice and coming to love virtue.

A life of taking on virtue and leaving vice behind is a real possibility if one begins to build a spiritual foundation. Our interior wound is so deep that we cannot sustain our own moral conversions. The building of virtue has to be constructed upon a foundation of grace. Practically, this means that we literally suffer the passing of our sins and the arrival of the "new man" in Christ. There is a spiritual suffering in moral conversion, sometimes so acute that it fills our bodies with torturous feelings of anguish. Through this suffering, grace is still with us, molding us to the crucified and resurrected Christ. As Jonathan Robinson has noted, "We want a new life, but the new life demands an effort on our part, and it is an effort in which we are reluctant to engage."[12]

As we become illumined by the sources of spiritual formation, we become disposed to listen to God's ways. We may not immediately relish what truth is bidding us to do, but in faith and with communal support we may soon engage the cross of new behavior patterns. To listen to God is not to become passive, but it is to become a discerning person. Moral listening entails actively searching for the truth in the light of one's ecclesial identity. To be illumined is to be one who searches and listens and responds to moral truth in ways not known before. To discern is to distinguish the voices of folly from those bearing truth. One can do this only by listening well to God, who is the source of one's true dignity.

One way that keeps this dignity before us is to keep the memory of sin alive. By this we do not mean that one keeps intellectually visiting the sins of the past, but that one keeps the memory of *the consequence* of sin alive in the mind in order to battle temptation. We Christians struggle through the purification process not so that we can return to the sinful way of life so recently rejected as being unfaithful to Christ. Purification readies us to move on to *a better life.* In the way of illumination, especially in the context of the eucharistic life, one's memories of sin no longer exist as temptations, but as sources of humility and gratitude. This healing work is found most profoundly in the liturgy. These healed memories work to keep us from returning to the slavery of sin. Before they are healed, however, the memory of sin can tempt us too easily to sin again; during this period, it is best to not visit the memory as it may elicit episodes that weaken moral resolve.

The Unitive Way

The new life given as a result of the purgative and illuminative ways is one of living out of the gifts of the Holy Spirit. It is a life of union with God. This does not mean the Christian enters some kind of definite state of constant emotional ecstasy. It simply means that over time, over a period of moving away from sin and taking on a life of virtue, we become open to the Spirit. In the spiritual life's most elegant moments, those who are predominantly led by the gifts of the Spirit will know a peace and surety of faith, hope, and love that no one can take from them. The predominant aspects of purgation and illumination have worked and continue to work their way on us so that we may come to a sure union with God and know purity of heart. Purity of heart is a single-minded intention to live for God and God alone. Again, we are to be prudent here—this does not mean we have to be disinterested in giving and receiving love from others. In fact, it is just the opposite. Those with a pure heart and who abide in the peace of union with God cannot but serve the needs of those whom they love. To become such a servant is one of the unspoken fruits of the Holy Spirit.

Jonathan Robinson speaks of the purity given after purgation and illumination in this way:

> By purity of conscience [De Caussade] means having no attachment to anything sinful; by purity of heart he means being detached even from objects that are apparently innocent....Purity of heart is a development of purity of conscience....If we are to love God and his creation with the same love with which God loves us, then we must be free....The culmination of the spiritual life is not the achievement of a static condition but a living twofold movement [of dying and rising] (Jn 12:23). It is the passage away from everything to find the love Who is infinitely greater and more wonderful than all His creation. Yet, having found Him in Himself, we then begin to love Him in all things. "The soul seems to be more God than soul," says St. John of the Cross, "and is truly God by participation."[13]

The expression of Saint John above is certainly one way of articulating the unitive aspect of Christian discipleship. The unitive aspect of the moral/spiritual life is seen alternately as a state of life and/or a mystical event. In its fullness it is simply a sign of a person's union with God in love. It is a foretaste of heaven. As we move through and around the aspects of purgation and illumination, we are being readied for heaven, for union with God. Believers develop a taste for heaven, become more comfortable living in the presence of God, delight in such a presence, and cannot believe that they could ever have lived otherwise. We cry out with Saint Augustine, "How late have I loved thee, O beauty so ancient yet so new, how late have I loved thee."[14]

In one sense we can say that in articulating the unitive aspect of Christian living, spiritual writers are making an effort to express the affective love of God over a more impersonal knowledge of truth. Purgation and illumination might be characterized as aspects of Christian living that focus upon where moral truth resides, whereas union responds to that reality by drawing the believer into the very origin of all truth, the love of God itself. In reality, however, love has always been active since the purgation dimension began, for it is love that finds us and invites us to come away from evil and receive the blessings of virtue (1 John 4:10). To distinguish too dramatically the realities of love of God and knowledge of truth is, in the end, not reflective of a real sacramental and moral life. To be one who embraces the moral good out of the theological virtues *is* to be a Christian. To be a Christian is to be one who has responded to the call of Christ to follow him along the way of purgation, illumination, and union. It is, in the end, to become simple. By this we mean that the Christian is the one who progressively comes willingly to host the indwelling Spirit of Christ, so that this Spirit can live Christ's life in such a one. To be simple is to be one who draws one's life from Christ's Spirit, manifesting this principle in virtuous living. It is at this point that the mystics begin to speak of infused virtues and gifts. This does not, however, mean that the Christian life begins to run on magical power. Bouyer clarifies what it does mean:

> This infused character of the virtues does not mean that their exercise requires no effort, but that this effort is to rest not on trust in ourselves but…on faith in grace that heals our nature.…And when [the virtues] are motivated by…the confident love, which, in us, is total self abandonment to the divine love [charity]—then [the virtues] gain a depth, a fullness of meaning and reality that the ancients never even suspected. Instead of simply setting us in our place in a static universe, [the infused virtues] draw us into the creative and saving impetus of Christ's love. Above all, in this

very love [the infused virtues] open us out to the contemplation...of that love which is the very life of God.[15]

The unitive way is best understood, finally, as the great gift of
presence from God to his beloved in ways that words fail to grasp
and whose reality is only glimpsed in the fruits of such a person's
own life. The person dwelling in the unitive aspect of the faith life
possesses a new conscience that draws its knowledge of truth from
the depths of this divine relationship. We come to live a mystical
obedience within which we allow God to be the sole master within
us (John 17:22–23).[16]

The three ways represent one model of moral/spiritual development in the Catholic tradition.[17] Its strength is in its respect for the
progressive development of the Christian in a way that tries to articulate a growing union between the human person and God. In
choosing this model, we too are simply trying to articulate a developmental view of moral/spiritual progress, one that acknowledges
that people come to God from different approaches and progress
toward holiness in their and God's own time. We now turn to see
how these very personal three ways relate to the more theological
reflections we made about the paschal mystery both in itself and as
it appears in the depths of pastoral life, the Eucharist.

How Do the Three Ways
Relate to the Paschal Mystery?

The three ways can be said to concretize and personalize a way
of living the paschal mystery. Of course, this way is closely aligned
with the sacramental life, as shall be noted below, but it is mainly a
life found in the daily relinquishing of sin and taking up of virtue.
This repudiating and affirming is always a task and a grace known
within the folds of everyday commitments and devotion to duty. In
other words, purgation and illumination are the stuff of Christian life;
union remains its lodestar and hope but cannot be a predicted result
of some spiritual technique. How can it be said that the three ways
personalize the paschal mystery?

As we described in chapter 1, the paschal mystery reveals to us
the true meaning of discipleship. "If any want to become my followers, let them deny themselves and take up their cross and follow me"

(Mark 8:34). Christ's paschal mystery reminds us that we are completely unable to bring about a conversion through our own efforts. Jesus' passion, death, and resurrection alone can effect a change in the depths of our humanity that, when applied to us individually, enables us to live as he lived. Christ wants to *enable* his followers to turn away from sin. It is the entire paschal mystery that carries the message that liberation from sin and death is possible. The purgative way encapsulates the work of this message. When one sets out on the course of discipleship, it is the evil of sin that is immediately confronted once the "yes" to Christ has been spoken. This is a confrontation that happens in the context of the "yes," not in isolation from it. In fact, it can be said that the "yes" to Christ is the necessary prerequisite for being able to battle pride, envy, greed, sloth, lust, gluttony, and anger as they emerge during the course of daily living. As John Paul II has written, "Jesus himself...becomes a living and personal law, who invites people to follow him; through the Spirit, he gives the grace to *share his own life* [emphasis added] and love and provides the love and provides the strength to bear witness to that love in personal choices and actions."[18]

Since the Holy Spirit lives within the believer, God is very close to us. In other words, this battle with sin is not removed from the presence of the paschal mystery—the mystery is *within* each person and in fact, over time, comes to *define* each Christian. In the purgative aspect of discipleship, this mystery-bearing Spirit is moving within us to heal our desire for certain sins, and within the illuminative process is encouraging us to "taste and see" (Ps 34:9) the joy of virtuous living.

Thomas Merton gives a good description of what happens to someone who is just entering the purgative process. His words below are prefaced with a narrative on how he spent his nights drinking in bars, preoccupied only with himself. He ends these reported evenings in the early morning waiting for a bus to take him home while watching other men go responsibly to work.

> The thing that depressed me most of all was the shame and despair that invaded my whole nature when the sun came up, and all the laborers were going to work: men healthy and awake and quiet, with eyes clear, and some rational purpose before them. This humiliation and sense of my own misery

and of the fruitlessness of what I had done was the nearest I could get to contrition....It proved nothing except that I was still, at least, morally alive; or rather that I had still some faint capacity for moral life in me. The term "morally alive" might obscure the fact that I was spiritually dead. I had been that long since!...I had at last become a true child of the modern world, completely tangled up in petty and useless concerns with myself, and almost incapable of even considering or understanding anything that was really important to my own true interests.[19]

Merton also captures a complementary description of the illuminative aspect of discipleship. This description occurs in the context of Merton having attended one of his first masses during his college days at Columbia University. He decides to leave the church after the homily.

It was liturgically fitting that I should kick myself out at the end of the Mass of the Catechumens....Anyway it was done. Now I walked down Broadway in the sun, and my eyes looked about me at a new world. I could not understand what it was that had happened to make me so happy, why I was so much at peace, so content with life for I was not yet used to the clean savor that came with an actual grace—indeed, there was no impossibility in a person's hearing and believing such a sermon and being justified, that is, receiving sanctifying grace in his soul as a habit, and beginning, from that moment, to live the divine and supernatural life for good and all....All I know is that I walked in a new world.[20]

For Merton, in the first instance the purgative aspect began in earnest when he identified sinful leanings within his self-centered habits. In so doing, the stirring of repugnance at such sin is clearly seen. In the latter quote he is beginning a journey of attraction to virtue, to worship, and to prayer. This attraction is clearly seen, and one can catch a glimpse of the joy he feels by moving through purgation to illumination. Of course, these two quotes are just illustrations of what purgation and illumination contain. We mention them here now because Merton captures the ordinariness of Christ's coming with healing and saving power. In the first instance grace comes at a bus station, and in the second at a daily Mass in the ordinary course of city life. The paschal mystery is diffusive and uses the things of this earth to carry its incredible message of conversion and joy: God is reaching out to the world, through the revelation of his Son, so that sin can be defeated by *Christ's own loving obedience.* This loving obedience is now ours to enter as well, through the many and varied gateways grace presents to us in the customary rounds of one's day.

It is unusual for a moral conversion to occur all at once; there is normally a preparation period in grace. As John Henry Newman asked, "Is not holiness the result of many patient, repeated efforts after obedience, gradually working on us, and first modifying then changing our hearts?"[21] In fact, Newman's comment is a perfect description of how the paschal mystery becomes lodged in one's heart and will. The Spirit looks for opportunities to become more deeply embedded within the believer during times of openness to truth—such as Merton standing dumb in the bus station before his own foibles, facing the virtue of other men who were committed to the practice of their vocational duties. Another opportunity for the Spirit came when Merton followed an inner urge to enter a Catholic church and witness the eucharistic liturgy in progress, staying just long enough to be penetrated by the gospel as it was unfurled in a simple homily.

The paschal mystery is incarnated again at these moments of cooperation with grace in our willingness to risk obedience. All purgation and illumination is dependent upon a lively and loving obedience that is being exercised within the will of a faith-filled believer. We cannot progress too far into the mystery of Christ if we do not go forward into Newman's "patient, repeated efforts after obedience." It is this movement of the loving will desiring to carry the kind of love that Christ bore that unlocks all the doors to true moral/spiritual living. If it is possible to pinpoint the kernel of conversion power that is the paschal mystery, we would assert that it is found in our sharing in Christ's obedience to love what is good and true, for what is good and true is a manifestation of what has been "secret for long ages" (Rom 16:25; Eph 3:5, 9; Col 1:26)—the creative, sustaining, and unifying love of the Father. It is this love that Christ came to bear, reveal, and ultimately share with all of humankind, which leads us to call this divine love by a new name, salvation. It is a love that heals and elevates the human so that a share in the divine life can be experienced, *even by creatures.*

Through the purgative and illuminative process we slowly come to realize our dignity before God. What God asks from us is a sustained life of love-imbued listening, expressed through discrete acts in varied contexts and situations. One's whole life, then, is marked by this turn toward a discriminating heart, one that discerns and then exclusively listens to the voice of the Lord. It is this openness to hear the Lord (obedience) that characterizes the believer as he or she discerns what discipleship demands. In order for one to be taken up into the paschal mystery via the three ways, this obedience must be sustained throughout the ensuing discipleship. Such obedience, however, is not oppressive, because Christ's mystery has become so interiorized that one comes to desire only what is of Christ and regret all that leads one astray. Only those opposed to the mystery, now made manifest in Christ, will find this rapt listening oppressive. This is not to say that the purgative aspect will not cause one hardship in following Christ; rather, most definitely the road from habitual sin to virtue will be one with suffering.

It is the hope for and at times foretaste of union with God, however, that keeps the suffering known in conversion from becoming a source of despair or cynicism. The unitive aspect of the Christian life can be known in more than one manner. Traditionally, the unitive way is the way of mystical ecstasy. That is still true, and it is given to those whom God so wills. This ecstatic gift is not a reward for tasks well done; it is simply a gracious movement of God's generosity, a hint at the eternal union to come for all those who persevere in faith, hope, and love. Mystical ecstasy, as well, does not exhaust nor even indicate proof of holiness within a person. Holiness is certainly union with God, but not all holy union yields mystical ecstasy.

Short of ecstasy, there are other minor, or "low level," mystical experiences that also affirm a person in God's friendship. Four examples are most relevant for our discussion of the three ways and their relationship to the paschal mystery. The first experience of union with God can be known in *consoling prayer.* This kind of prayer is sustained by a grace of ever-deepening desire for prayer, and it sees its fruit in longer periods of time in actual prayer. Within this prayer, one is graced with peaceful feelings of contentment about being in the presence of God. One actually likes being in prayer; being so is no longer carried as a duty but is embraced eagerly as a privileged moment. Like Christ in prayer, one is ardent in listening to God and following God's truth wherever it leads.[22]

Another level of union with God is known in the experience of having *prayer come upon a believer* during the normal course of a day. It is as if God alights upon us as a friend might unexpectedly visit out of love. One could be doing the most ordinary of tasks, and suddenly the mind is filled with gratitude to God for the providence shown, or with an intercession for a beloved family member who is ill, or with sighs of lament that erupt over one's own sin or the sinfulness of our human condition. No matter the content of prayer, what is crucial is that God is visiting us with the spirit of prayer and we are welcoming it without delay. This kind of experience indicates a certain union with God that is nourished and treasured with each similarly ensuing prayer encounter.

There is also the *union known through sacramental living*. This does not usually have a deep affectivity about it, but objectively it is the clearest form of union. Surely the reception of the sacraments by believers who are well-disposed to receive them is the clear sign of our desire for union with God, as the sacraments' very existence indicates God's eternal love for us. To enter the prayer of the sacraments is to enter the paschal mystery in its fullness for we who still travel the earth in time. We can get no closer to the mystery than through the sacraments. It is especially important to note this for those who are married. The state of sacramental marriage allows a couple to deepen their love for one another and for Christ's salvific heart with each choice that is made in favor of the welfare of one's spouse. Here the paschal mystery truly comes to make its home in ordinary life, one full of fidelity to child-rearing, economic responsibilities, sexual love, service to neighbor and community, and friendship between man and woman. One also finds this close intimacy with God through fidelity to the duties of Holy Orders and the baptized life of single Catholics. Each of these vocational sacraments is oriented to the depths of the paschal mystery by participating in the Eucharist and frequenting the sacrament of reconciliation.

Finally, there is a union when *acting on the judgment of conscience* despite sure knowledge of the suffering that will accompany the doing of moral truth. When believers follow their conscience and enact behavior embodying moral truth, they can be assured of a certain union with God. This witness to the fruit of listening to the prayerful conscience will be affirmed by society, or on occasion this same obedience to moral truth can cause the agent untold suffering if the particular truth being obeyed is threatening to those who benefit from it being ignored. It is the Spirit working within us that frees us to obey the conscience by appeal, not coercion. In standing with the truth of conscience, we are being grasped by the Spirit of truth, who leads us to the deepest realities of the paschal mystery. "The Spirit searches hearts…and intercedes for the holy ones according to God's will" (Rom 8:27). These realities encompass the core of the paschal mystery in Christ's own loving obedience to the will of God. In this obedience, and in this alone, depends the whole mystery of salvation. In some way we can even speak of salvation for nonbelievers in and through their faithful following of conscience, so much does this obedience to moral truth carry divine things.

Moral Theology Viewed from the Side of Mystery

As noted above, it is the paschal mystery as encountered within the eucharistic liturgy, and assisted by the sacrament of reconciliation, that is the place par excellence for moral formation and conversion.[23] By living out of this power, drawing from it, and worshipping God in and through this mystery, one is not simply forming a generically ethical mind, but "the mind of Christ" (1 Cor 2:16). As Columba Marmion beautifully summarizes:

> If we desire, He will be in us as the agonizing Saviour, who by His wonderful submission to His Father's good pleasure obtains for us the grace to bear our daily crosses; He will be the Divine Risen Lord who grants us to detach ourselves from all that is earthly, to "live unto God" more generously and fully; He will be in us the Victor who gloriously ascends into heaven and draws us after Him that we may already dwell there by faith, hope and holy desire. Christ thus contemplated and received is Christ living His mysteries over again in us.…[T]he most perfect participation in this divine mystery of the altar is sacramental communion.[24]

In these ideas of Marmion lie the seeds for developing a *full* moral theology as viewed from the side of mystery. By this we mean a moral theology that begins and is sustained by the mysteries of Christ's life, and his promises to live his life in us as we travel through our time on earth. If we approach the Eucharist in faith, then we will pass through the senses to that newness of life both promised by and prefigured in the resurrection of Christ (Phil 3:10). Again Marmion expresses this succinctly:

> The mysteries of Jesus have this characteristic that they are ours as much as they are His....It is an inexhaustible source of confidence for a soul that loves Jesus to know that He Himself unites her intimately with each of His mysteries....How is it that Christ's mysteries are our mysteries? First of all, because Christ lived them for us, [second] that in all of [his mysteries] Christ shows Himself to us as our Exemplar....Each of His mysteries is the revelation of His virtues....The Eternal Father accepts us only inasmuch as He sees in us a resemblance to His Son....[It] is to this very resemblance that, from all eternity, He predestined us. There is no other form of holiness for us than that which Christ showed to us....There is, finally, a third reason...which makes Christ's mysteries our own....[T]he Eternal Father saw us with His Son in each of the mysteries lived by Christ. [Christ] wills that the union which, by grace, attaches Him to His disciples, should be the same as that which, by nature, identifies Him with His Father....All that He has [virtues] is ours; we are rich with His riches, holy with His holiness....It is true that in their historical, material duration, the mysteries of Christ's terrestrial life are now past; but their virtue remains, and the grace which gives us a share therein is always operating.[25]

Truly, the riches of a Catholic moral life as known through and in the paschal mystery are present in this description by Dom Marmion. Christ came to live his life *for us;* in so doing, he became a *model for our own life of virtue;* and finally, we see in Christ our own unity with God, and we seek to fulfill our eternal destiny by *living united to Christ.* As Marmion says, "if we desire He will be in us," living his mysteries, drawing and gathering us into the "new creation" (2 Cor 5:17).

By a *full moral theology* we do not mean that every answer to every concrete moral question is automatically resolved by approaching ethical discernment from mystery. The minds that tackle concrete moral problems from such an approach, however, will be capable of discerning religiously and not simply by the accessible secular methods of the current culture (laws, economic principles of consumer choice, politically correct ideologies, and so on). By *full* we do not mean full of all answers—we mean the fullness of Christ; we mean that all moral query is placed before and within the paschal mystery, not before a code of law or the politically current taxonomy of dos and don'ts. Our approach yields a way of moral thinking that is explicitly based upon the spiritual side of Christian life. In fact we hope that this book articulates a way of moral formation that is not separate from spirituality but *is a spirituality,* and a spirituality that *is a moral theology.* We achieve this by keeping our thinking close to the paschal mystery and the Eucharist. In this way the believer has a method of shaping conscience by worship and doctrine in order to discern moral questions from religious faith. Such a person will discern between virtue and vice out of the depths of mystery, community, and with due reverence for truths already defined by the teaching authority of the church, which were themselves discerned out of the depths of a communal reason filled with the grace of worship.

The Conscience and Moral Formation in the Three Ways

As we approach and participate in the paschal mystery, our *desires* are transformed, as is our *intellect in its orientation toward truth—being the person of Christ—*as is *our ease in choosing* the good and holy. We learn what is morally true from the perfect man: Jesus Christ. In him we are led to communion with God, and because of such communion, we are also led to true fidelity to the human identity. In *Gaudium et Spes* no. 22 we read this: "In reality it is only in the mystery of the Word made flesh that the mystery of man truly becomes clear....Conformed to the image of the Son who is the first-born of many brothers the Christian man receives the 'first fruits of the Spirit' (Rom 8:23) by which he is able to fulfill the new law of love. By this Spirit...the whole man is inwardly renewed, right up to the 'redemption of the body' (Rom 8:23)."

1. *"Our desires are transformed: He has come to live his life for us"* *(The Purgative Way).* To realize that Christ came for us and for our

salvation is to begin to grasp what is vitally important about divine love. From such an awareness, gratitude and humility emerge as fruits within our own character, as we grow in desire to serve and please such a one who would give all for us. A notable sign that the kingdom is breaking into time and pulling us forward toward the eschaton is a person's rejection of sin and the establishment by God of infused virtue within this person's character. Truly to live oriented toward God in worship and come before him seeking purity, and offering for healing the impurity still within us, is to know the life of a "new creation." Following John 6, Dom Marmion concludes that the Eucharist is the bread of life because "it places in our very bodies the germ of the resurrection."[26] It is the Eucharist that "excites charity and sustains fervour," rendering the soul "prompt and devoted in God's service." Marmion summarizes his point in this way, "Christ, ever living, acts in silence, but sovereignly in the innermost depths of the soul in order to transform it into Himself; that is the most precious effect of this heavenly food; he that eateth of my flesh and drinketh my blood abideth in Me and I in him."[27] As Marmion alludes, the mystery of the resurrection should be a central truth upon which to build meditations on moral living. If this is true, then the Eucharist, wherein the entire paschal mystery is laid before us, is unquestionably the chief source of moral transformation. The moral life in Christ is powered by the resurrected Christ—sharing new life with his mystical body.

In medieval spirituality, saints would attest to this newness of desire in phrases that reflected their coming to see that what was once sweet (a particular vice) is now bitter. Concretely, the moral life changes when desire changes, and it is Christ's grace that assists in that change, leaving one amazed at one's past. "How could I have possibly thought or believed that such a vice would lead to my happiness? How could that habit have been thought 'sweet'?"

The movement from desiring vice to desiring and recognizing virtue might be a long one. This is why so many spiritual masters counsel patience and gentleness with the self in the midst of moral conversion. This advice is granted by the best spiritual directors not because they are lax guides, but rather it is given to thwart any capitulation to temptation in the face of inevitable suffering during the process of rejecting vice. If one is comfortable with a life of gluttony, lust, or envy, that comfort level simply indicates how deeply imbedded such viciousness has become. To learn the bitterness of vice may take awhile as the sweetness of its memory still lingers close to the affections. There is pleasure in vicious behavior or none of us would do it. Changing the will, mind, and affect in relation to the memory of such pleasure or rewards can be hard work. The only *defeat* in moral conversion, however, is giving up the challenge to have our desires change and succumbing to the power of vice as "inevitable."

The bringing of sinful desires to the mystery of the Eucharist represents the genius of those who want to become saints. To offer these unruly desires for transformation into the desires of Christ places the worshipper at the very core of why Christ came "for us and for our salvation." Our desires are only changed according to that in which we participate. If one continues to participate in the habits of greed, for example, and places worship alongside this habit, progress in becoming generous will be slow to nonexistent. Again, entry into the mysteries of Christ does not magically replace evil with good, but it does begin the work of divine-human cooperation in the emergence of the believer as a "new creation." For our desires to change, we have to begin to participate in the virtue we seek to inhabit us. This is where patience and gentleness toward self come in; otherwise we are at risk of stagnating in hopelessness. The grace, the living divine force of resurrection power found within worship will change us, but it will be a work in progress. God wants the change rendered in us to go to the roots of our character, not painted on as a thin veneer.

In order for the desire for virtue to take root at the core of our character, the desires for the old objects of pleasure, power, and security have to be scoured. This is the work of a life devoted to the Eucharist. In having our desires altered, we are leaving our taste for this world and developing a taste for heaven. The affections bind us to what we love, to that with which we seek union. To have an affection for vice weakens, and can ultimately destroy, our capacity to recognize the holy. There is, then, urgency to the task of bringing our vicious desires to the healing power of worship. In so doing we gain a sense of what is good and what is evil, thus avoiding a spiraling down into moral blindness. Becoming a saint is not natural; it is an acquired grace.[28] This grace affects the intellect in its judgment of right and wrong and affects our attractions to proper and good ends.

At the core of having our desires purified is the virtue of humility. In order to sustain the turn from sin to holiness, we have to have a sense of our own place in God's world. Humility opposes the proud person who fails to acknowledge God as the source and center of all power to change. The humble person knows that it is God's life lived in him that matters most of all. Our efforts to surrender to grace meet God's power and will to save; in that meeting the humble one yields to divine power and knows herself as a "new creation." In a real way it is the task-gift of humility that contains the core of the purgative way. As Marmion says, "humility, in achieving the work of removing the obstacles opposed to divine unity, takes, from this point of view, first rank."[29] Humility removes the obstacles to living as a friend of God first and foremost by placing the person before God in truth. Humble people cannot bring themselves to be anything but honest in the face of God's love. To the humble person, it is simply necessary to admit limits, faults, mistakes, and sin directly and with no rationalizations, excuses, or explanations. We are what we are before God and nothing more. If this virtue takes root in us, we are truly on the way to moral/spiritual renewal.

The process of having one's desires changed through the working of the virtue of humility makes up the core of the purgative way. In the purgative way, as we have seen, we move from vice to virtue. We let go of sin and form a heart eager to listen for moral truth. Our desires need training, however, and thus the illuminative way awaits as a concrete source for such formation: Christ in his Word of truth.

2. "Truth is a Person": Christ is the Model for All Virtue (The Illuminative Way). Once we begin to realize that desires ground what we choose, and that our choices define who we become, we go looking for one who is well-ordered in desire and in judgment of conscience so as to see such a life fulfilled. Of course, for the Christian, it is Christ who presents himself as *the* model of all virtue. Clinging to the person of Christ, not to concepts, is the way to truth. This is not anti-intellectualism but the definition of intellect itself: we put the mind at the service of what we believe in and love. Christ is the final word on the truth of virtue. If he is the truth, then he is the embodiment of one who is good, because truth and goodness cannot be separated. The mind, which seeks truth, ultimately seeks truth so that a person *can live in it*. To live in truth is to live *in Christ*, and to come to faith is to invite Christ to live *in you*.

With Christ, the exemplar of all virtue, the believer seeks to find a door into Christ's mind. What does it mean to think like Christ and live like Christ? This is the guiding question for the passion of saints. This passion leads believers to seek out the sources of conscience formation. We locate the scriptures, the signs and symbols of salvation in worship, the lives of the saints, and the works of service toward those in need. In this way, Christians seek intimacy with Christ and draw strength from his presence in these arenas. The believer also seeks to rest with Christ in contemplation and have his presence pervade the soul, so that the public works of worship, service, and study can have their roots in intimacy with the divine. In this way the former is nourished by the latter, and worship, service, and learning never become ways to self-promotion or self-destruction, but simply *a way through life* as one who has been illumined by Christ.

The distinction between imitating and following Christ has been written about many times. Suffice it to say that we *are not* called to mimic Christ in his personal acts (e.g., live in Nazareth, work with our hands, and so on). We are, however, called *literally to follow him to the source of his obedience.* We are called to host the Spirit of Christ and have it blow where it will, trusting always that Christ now takes up residence in his body, the church, traveling through and pervading the world well beyond the confines of Palestine. In this way the church becomes the new body of Christ doing those "greater works" that Christ himself foretold (John 14:12). Thus, there is no sense of mimicking, only following Christ, each to his own vocational fount, containing within it the spiritual hydration needed to sustain the inevitable crosses that such commitments will bring. By living this kind of life, Christ comes to meet us to empower our fidelity to vocation. As he would not turn away from his Father's voice, neither do we wish to listen to anyone but him who is truth itself. We therefore hope that such a listening, discerning stance will bring us to embrace the virtues needed for "a life worthy of the calling to which [we] have been called" (Eph 4:1).

In order for Christ to be the model of all virtue, one has to see within Christ the "perfect man." It is not, however, simply an intellectual recognition of Christ's moral goodness that empowers a person to become "another Christ." Such a moral/spiritual transformation is beyond imitation—it is received as a *gift that is practiced.* To say this is to say that the moral virtues take root in those Christians who see the spiritual life as the foundation for securing the sustained exercise of virtues over the course of a lifetime. To *practice a gift,* we are called to allow the gift to affect our character formation. In the matter of Christ as model of moral virtue, we are not dealing with ascertaining rules gleaned from Christ's life; we are practicing spiritual ways of becoming more vulnerable before the person of Christ.

Analogically, a husband does not love his wife in order to discern rules of behavior; he loves her for who she is and then conforms his behavior to the nature of that love. In this way his behavior flows freely to serve her good, and he is vulnerable, as well, to her loving ways so that he might incorporate her ways into his own life. Here we see the dynamics of love defining behavior that is in accord with that love. In the same manner, one sees Christ in his divine identity as worthy of love and moves toward Christ for who he is, not for the discovery of rules of behavior. In this friendship with Christ, how-ever, we learn of love and so wish to act upon that knowledge, bring-ing us closer to Christ and to behavior befitting such a friendship. Certainly we may need to listen to others who have endeavored to love this way as well (e.g., the saints), just as an earnest husband might seek advice from his father or his respected married friends. These sought-out "rules" are helpful, but they must always be brought back into the context of one's own loving vocation to *this* particular wife, in *this* particular circumstance. There are obvious universal behaviors that need to be avoided in both divine and human love relationships: infidelity, failure in communication and avoidance of self-revelation, neglect, and even more obvious, any behavior that seeks willfully to destroy communion with the beloved.

Learning virtue from Christ is cast within a context of love for who Christ is, so that who he is may render the believer vulnerable to transformation, a transformation graced and willed, gifted and enacted. Loving Christ through the worship of the church, spiritual reading, and service to those in need creates a character deeply open to hosting the divine life. In this openness to host the living God, our movement toward becoming good and holy is solidified. Our holi-ness is not complete, but we have reached the secure ground where fertile growth in the moral/spiritual life can truly be sustained.

3. *"It becomes easier to choose virtue as one united to Christ" (The Unitive Way).* Throughout this book we have been focusing upon the

paschal mystery being lived within us. The practical payoff of such a truth is found in the growing ease with which one chooses and enacts the moral good. This ease has replaced a former struggle, because now one is empowered to live virtuously by the divine life. Christ is the only route to happiness, the only route, in other words, to being faithfully human. Faith in Christ allows the person who desires virtuous living to bring that desire to satisfaction in holiness.

Eager for holiness and virtue, and beholding Christ as our prime exemplar, we are readied to enact our desire for truth in, through, and with Christ. Here we see where the moral life becomes equated with the life of prayer. Out of one's union with God, decisions are made that reflect such a union between the soul and Christ, who is truth. Moral decision-making becomes the fruit of conversation with the indwelling Spirit. Such decisions reflect the rapt listening of one who discerns action from within a matrix of personal love for God. We open ourselves up to be affected by the indwelling Spirit, and we expect the truth known in such affection to be our way to holiness.

This union in prayer is not exhausted in the soul of any one believer. This whole process of allowing the paschal mystery to be lived within the body also includes and depends upon it being welcomed in the body of the church as well. Not only is the unitive way a way for individuals to discern and enact the truths found through prayer, but it is the way for the community to articulate moral truths as well. Unless cynicism or corruption reigns in the church during any one epoch, the normal route to defining moral truth for the entire community is through the love-imbued reason of the bishops in union with the pope. There is no oracle for ecclesial leadership to follow, but there is the guidance of the indwelling Spirit of Christ who promised never to abandon church leadership in its mission to identify moral truth for each age. In those areas where no clear moral truth is articulated by the bishops, the community endeavors to discern its consequent behavior through consultation, *lectio divina,* and shared prayer. If we can speak of community holiness, each diocese, parish, or domestic church can become more and more united to Christ as a body. Holiness is collective, therefore, when each member yearns to practice virtue from within his or her united commitment to draw life and strength from the paschal mystery through the workings of sacramental living.[30]

The unitive way holds the key to the joy of moral/spiritual living. One can speak of being dead to the world and alive in Christ as the fruits of desire and the love of truth lead a community to union with the holy, experienced now as ease and peace in the choosing of virtue. This joy will be recognized as a gift of the Spirit for those willing to pass through the changing of desires and the school of truth. Similar to but not without real distinction, one can say that those with pure hearts are like those who know contemplative prayer; for those who pursue the truth of virtue, willing what is morally good becomes an act chosen from within a habit of love. Within such a community of persons, following the dictates of conscience "is now like one to whom water is brought, so that he drinks peacefully, without labor."[31] Such persons emit joy over being enmeshed in virtue. They are at once compassionate toward sinners, but also somewhat surprised that sin remains a real option for fellow believers. Such is the disposition they have garnered through growth in the love of God.

Conscience Formation Viewed from the Side of Mystery

Above we noted that Marmion succinctly summarized the three ways in the context of the paschal mystery by elucidating:

> If we desire, He will be in us as the agonizing Saviour, who by His wonderful submission to His Father's good pleasure obtains for us the grace to *bear our daily crosses;* He will be the Divine Risen Lord who grants us to detach ourselves from all that is earthly, to *"live unto God" more generously and fully;* He will be in us the Victor who gloriously ascends into heaven and *draws us after Him* that we may already dwell there by faith, hope and holy desire. Christ thus contemplated and received is Christ living His mysteries over again in us....[T]he most perfect participation in this divine mystery of the altar is sacramental communion. [All emphasis has been added.][32]

The "grace to bear our daily crosses" is the purgative movement of conversion, opening up to the illuminative, expressed as "liv[ing] unto God more generously," culminating in the unitive, "the Victor who gloriously ascends into heaven and draws us after Him that we may already dwell there by faith, hope and holy desire." The formation of the virtuous Christian needs to inhabit these three mysteries and so become identified with them in the making of judgments of conscience. Moving beyond what we meditated upon above—the changing of desires, the falling in love with truth, and the new ease with which one comes to make moral judgments—we now have to consider the actual formation of a mystery-imbued conscience and its relevant application to daily pastoral life. We will do this under the three expressions of Marmion that make up his summary of the three ways in the context of the paschal mystery: bearing, living, and drawing.

Bearing the Cross as Conscience Formation

The conscience of a believer is formed deep within the folds of fidelity to ordinary daily duties. The primary energy of daily formation centers around the skills needed for listening and discerning in order for one to remain faithful to one's sacramental vocation. From within fidelity to vocation we learn the cross as Christ lives this mystery in us and for us. Specifically, the cross entails the disposition to meet evil with love. It is a habit of living out of resurrection power, of disarming evil by yielding to the new life arising out of fidelity to God's goodness. In the face of evil, this disposition can place the believer in the throes of suffering. This suffering is known by those who wrestle with the choice of virtue within a context of temptation. Christ teaches us the correct choices from within our ecclesially centered hearts, thus sustaining us in our vocations. Within each choice to suffer goodness in the face of temptation to evil, the believer grows in the capacity to bear the cross.

The conscience begins, then, to bear the marks of the cross. The mind is readied, and in holy persons is eager, to search out virtue when evil tempts. In this way we are marked by the cross; we have come to possess a mind that judges good and evil from within the mystery of Christ's own obedience. A mind imprinted with loving, rapt listening to the truth is one that spiritually encapsulates the stigmata. Even if one does not physically bear the marks of Christ, as did Francis of Assisi or Pio of Pietrelcina, one is capable of bearing the stigmatic conscience. Out of such a mind, one discerns good and evil from within the Spirit-filled obedience that led Christ to the cross of meeting evil with love. This conscience imperceptibly develops within a matrix of sacramental living, *lectio divina,* and service to those in need.

One might also speak of a communal conscience. By this expression we mean the memory in the collective tradition of the community that acts both through prophetic persons and small groups of persons, and inheres in the communal texts and worship rituals. This communal conscience does not effect any specific moral judgments for any one individual, as that can only be accomplished within and by particular persons. It does, however, raise questions about current behavior within church or culture, challenging the community not to lose sight of the paschal mystery and the value of meeting evil with love. This communal conscience of memory is essential as cultures can find it difficult to be clear about their own fidelity to truth from within the commitments of day-to-day life. For such a memory to be effective, there needs to be a prerequisite openness to learn on the part of persons in community, even from unexpected sources.

The voice of the communal culture may coalesce within one's conscience and urge one to speak out in the name of fidelity to Christian identity. Such prophets are both in touch with their own conscience and possess such a conscience deeply familiar with the collective mission of the church, and so they come to speak out of the tradition with their own voice. Whether the ecclesial authorities recognize such a voice as being legitimate in its origin and direction is, of course, both the gift and burden of the church and of being a prophet as well. In carrying the gift of seeing truth before others, one truly knows the stigmatic conscience at work.

The communal conscience also inheres in the traditional texts of the church. Here the scholar plays a familiar role of bringing both old and new things from the storeroom (Matt 13:52). Without the work of scholars in all fields, the ecclesial memory of the dignity of the church might simply be lost in the swirl of current concerns. Albeit not needed for daily consultation by bishops and other church leaders, those who possess the skills to retrieve the memory of the community through study truly preserve the sources for individual conscience formation as well. Without the traditions of past holiness preserved and understood, the individual conscience of any one epoch would lose its way by the rush of daily affairs.

Even if one prays daily for light, such light is not guaranteed simply by such prayer alone. Many people pray fervently and still miss seeing their own personal cooperation with sin. Because such is the case, welcoming the prophetic voice, and the forgotten or dismissed voices of our full tradition, assists individuals in avoiding the blind spots within their own comfortable world view. The formation of conscience from the side of mystery recognizes these two sources of renewal, because it sees that Christ himself embodied such sources himself.

Living unto God More Generously

The trust that grows between a believer and God enables bold decision-making based upon a history of divine providence. "God guided my conscience in the past; God will be there for me now." This trust takes the form of a prayer, a communication between the one searching for virtue and the God who establishes and embodies goodness itself. We can afford to trust God more, give our problems over to God, and be confident in a decision-making process that is immersed in prayer and in prudent counsel from holy believers.

God's own generosity of self-gift fuels one's own capacity to entrust the self to the discernment process. We come to acknowledge that since God is living his life in us, he wants our well-being. God is seen as an ally in the search for happiness. God becomes a real companion at the table of life. Believers feed off the divine wisdom served within the stigmatic conscience and delight in the sureness of God's presence within. Of course, there is no *infallible instruction* given from within by the Spirit-soaked mind, but believers have the surety of the Spirit's *unfailing presence*. If Christians discern wrongly, the trust in God's presence ought not to be shattered, as the link between truth and our correct perception of it can be forged again through prayer, fasting, and counsel.

> We know by Revelation that God wills us to deliver ourselves to His action of grace expressly, to empty and to open ourselves so as to undergo it; and that, in these moments of a specific personal contact with God...conditions are given for an influx of grace....The deepest effect on our being emanates from our contemplative surrender to God.... Whenever we offer ourselves to God in thematical awareness...of Christ alone; whenever we lose ourselves in the

> vision of His face and dispose ourselves to be permeated by
> His light, He stamps our essence with His seal.[33]

The more we yield to the truth that God in Christ is absolutely trust-
worthy, the more we will be sealed with his mysterious presence. To
be sealed is to be made secure, fastened to the truth as known in
God. It leads one to choose actions that only convey such sealing by
God. Our actions become a witness to divine activity for others, and
our behavior can be seen as exemplary for those who also wish to be
sealed by and fastened to the mystery of Christ's holy and loving
obedience to the Father. We are made generous in doing good by the
life of Christ dwelling within and thus our actions, and the character
from which they flow, become signs of a crucified life, of cooperating
with the essence of Christ's crucifixion ministry of "drawing all
people to myself" (John 12:32).

Drawing Us after Him

Where in fact does Christ draw us? It would seem that his way
of the cross draws us ahead, draws us along with him into a heavenly life. There is an eschatological dimension to Christian moral living. By grace, by yielding to the Spirit, we are emblems of what is to
come. Surely, we are not made complete, but it can be said that
those who desire holiness and enact the truth that claims the conscience come to testify that resurrection power is real. It is these followers of Christ that we look to as models of freedom. One is only
free by being bound to what is good, loving, and true. The end result
of all Christian moral living is to know such freedom in and through
Christ, who is truth, love, and goodness itself. The very person of
Christ reaches out to his members still living in history so that they
may know his power as the one who is the way, the truth, and the
life. In reality, then, Christ is the embodiment of the three ways for
his people. As we struggle to move out of sinful patterns of choosing,
Christ shows us the way to purification. As we seek enlightenment to
secure our nascent love of virtue, he stands for us as truth, and as
we finally receive the destiny of our dignity as ones beloved by God,
he shares his divine life with us and brings us into everlasting union.
Christ has gone ahead to prepare a place for us. That is the promise
and fulfillment of his paschal mystery for us. The beginning of such

life in heaven is prefigured here in Christ's own power to draw us out of sin into "his marvelous light" (1 Pet 2:9).

Observations

1. The psychologist Charles Shelton defines conscience as: "Judgments based on an internal sense of oughtness (how I should live, or what I must do) that is the result of a life history that incorporates who I am, who I am becoming, and who I desire to be."[34] We have outlined the "life history" of the conscience of a believer above and in the previous chapters. Who a Christian is, is becoming, and desires to be is specifically incorporated into the mysteries of Christ. That is what defines the Christian conscience as such, and that is the living source from which the will draws strength and the mind inspiration in the face of temptation to go against conscience. The actual choosing to abide by the truth as one knows it can be and very often is a complicated emotional experience. The mysteries of Christ act therefore to center the person, especially one who is not yet mature in holiness, who is so struggling to faithfully choose the good. The struggle to follow conscience might be so striking that the person has literally to kneel and pray for strength, or reach out to a fellow believer for support, or cling to the Word of God as a ready source of God's providential presence. Only a person who has not tried to leave vice behind and take up the ways of holiness would think such a transition is pacific. Thus, the conscience needs concrete formation in the ways of the saints, in the ways of entering the Garden of Gethsemane, which here means the conscience. Christ literally threw himself down on the ground in terror before the prospect of dying (Mark 14:35); we too can expect a full emotional struggle in going forward in fidelity to our moral dying. Will I or will I not act against who I am, who I am becoming, and who I desire to be? These were Christ's questions, albeit unspoken, in the Garden of Gethsemane, and they are ours as well.

The stigmatic conscience can and will judge evil always to be wrong and loving truth always to be the way of life. Enacting this way is the work of our will and the fruit of our character formed by worship, study, and sacramental grace within the context of parish community. The further removed we are from the mysteries, and from others who so want to live them, the less our conscience reasons out of our deepest sacramental identity. Not to aspire to such a reasoning conscience is to miss the whole point of the sacramental life in relation to our growth in virtue, for to reason out of mystery is to have that mind liberated for discipleship thinking, a reality praised and sought after by the saints as being a participation in the mind of Christ. This kind of mind bears the brand marks of Christ, and so has become vulnerable to the ways of truth and fidelity as tasted by Christ in the Garden of Gethsemane.

Therefore, the conscience formed by the eucharistic mystery is one that calls the believer to embrace weakness. We are not to labor for virtue under our own power, but with the same divine strength that assisted Christ we are to rise again from the ground of Gethsemane and go forward in fidelity. To embrace such weakness is to live in reality, the reality of knowing the power of evil and the reality of knowing one's own vulnerability to succumb to such power. Christ comes to our aid and beckons us to empty our egoistic leanings and welcome the only power that can overcome evil, grace.

2. All of our moral discernment, therefore, begins and ends within the matrix of fidelity to identity. From within such an atmosphere, we act to secure our identity and deepen our fidelity to and communion with God and others. Concrete actions need to be taken within the structures of parish and family life to facilitate such discernment. Such actions include, but are not exhausted by, the traditional methods of adult faith formation, retreats, catechetical homilies, and other effective adult formation methodologies. The real core of such formation is the imparting of wisdom on the topics of listening for truth, discerning the voices claiming to bear truth, and structuring liturgical, pious, and service-oriented opportunities needed to facilitate enacting the moral truth. All of this is energized around the key formation question, "Does your presence at Sunday worship indicate a willingness to have your identity ultimately claimed by the paschal mystery?"

3. Being so claimed gives the moral life a foundation of hope. In the Old Testament, at certain points, death is seen as a punishment for sin. What happens, however, to those who die in the service of virtue or holiness? Slowly the Judeo-Christian tradition began to note that those who so died would be restored to life by the God who founded the covenant of life. Analogically, then, we can argue that those who die to selfishness in the service of life and truth will be

restored to life as well. In other words, the life we think we are los-
ing in the taking up of virtue and the sloughing off of vice is the loss
not of something valuable but of the simply familiar. Yes, something
is really dying, but something else is coming to be, as guaranteed by
the nature of God, who is only life, truth, and love. Thus, those who
convert from vice will come to "live again" within and by the power
of Christ's mysterious resurrection power. It is this kind of hope that
assists us in getting through the conversion from sin to virtue. It is
also the imagery needed deep within the conscience to sustain our
fidelity to truth and continue to internalize the paschal mystery. Only
the mystery *internalized* has the power to be called forth when
needed in order to guide the believer into living its realities.

4. We began this chapter by noting with Marmion "that Christ's
mysteries are our mysteries."[35] It is crucial, therefore, that Catholic
moral theology emphasize the idea of imitation of Christ. By this we
mean what Louis Gillon meant by the word *imitation:* an intense freedom to participate in the virtues of Christ, grounded in contemplation.[36] The way of imitation is the way of following Christ to the source
of his obedience to the Father, as was noted above. The source of his
obedience can be characterized as the heart of our participatory
engagement in his life. In other words, when we present the moral life
as one of participation in the mysteries of Christ, we are saying that to
become virtuous as a Christian one must desire to have Christ's freedom reign in one's and the community's center. It is Christ's freedom
before moral evil that he wants to gift us with most of all, from an ethical perspective. Without such freedom we cannot imitate him, we
cannot go where he went: into the life of rapt listening to the Father's
voice, even if it killed him. The paschal/eucharistic life then becomes
the way to freedom, the way to serenity before vices overcome and
struggle before vices still needing to be tamed. To be free in Christ,
then, is not to be without suffering but to be without confusion. It is to
be without confusion of desire (one wants to be holy) and, after a time,
without confusion over choices to be made as well (after discernment
the truth will claim us). Discernment is necessary because there really
are new choices to be made by individuals and communities; and such
choices by their nature are not self-evident even with a knowledge of
Christ and his mysteries. Thus, to imitate Christ is to follow a course
wherein we open ourselves to him living his obedience in us; in allowing this life to be lived in us we become free.

Concluding Remarks

What then does it mean to have a mind formed by mystery? It means abandoning oneself to the mysterious reign of Christ within the church, world, and individual heart. This abandonment bears fruit in the silent workings of Christ deep within the conscience. These workings are silent, meaning there are little or no continuously noticeable affective movements within such a person. Christ is working to change a person's conscience from within but in such a way that grace accords nature and human development its due. In the context of the moral/spiritual life, then, grace includes the entire offering of God as saving Lord: pardon for sin (justifying grace); help to overcome temptation and to do good (actual grace); new life in the Holy Spirit, which is a participation in divine life (sanctifying grace); and the divine indwelling (uncreated grace).

The moral life is a matter of depth and of being bound to a grace-filled sacramental manner of life. All mystical living begins in an encounter, one's and/or a community's meeting of God's presence. Within this meeting are born the theological virtues that then cultivate the moral virtues. Mystical moral living is experienced not in a rush of emotion but in a consistent pattern of seeking the good as it presents itself to a conscience imbued with the mysteries of Christ. To be holy is to be related to the divine source of all morality known in the sacramental life and in the faithful discharging of one's ordinary vocational duties. To look beyond these concrete realities is to miss the very door to sharing in the divine life.[37]

CHAPTER FIVE

Discerning Out of Mystery

[T]his much we do know, and can reasonably expect, that if a man honestly wants to follow the way of Christ and, as it were, opens his own personality to God, he will without any doubt receive something of the Spirit of God. As his capacity grows and as his own channel of communication widens, he will receive more. John goes so far as to call this the receiving of God's own heredity (1 John 3:9). This does not, of course, turn a man into a spiritualist medium! The man's own real self is purified and heightened, and though he will come to bear a strong family likeness to Christ he will, paradoxically enough, be more "himself" than he was before.

J. B. Phillips
Your God Is Too Small[1]

Christ's paschal mystery lies at the very heart of the Christian message. We share in that mystery through our participation in the church's sacramental worship, especially when we break bread together at Eucharist. When we gather around the table of the Lord, we proclaim our faith to the world and affirm the centrality of the Christ event for our lives. Because we are members of his body, Christ's story has now become our story—and our stories, his. We open our personalities to Christ, and he opens his personality to us. The Spirit of Christ dwells in our hearts, blesses us with its many gifts, and enables us to become more fully ourselves. As a result, the liturgy of the Eucharist spills over into the liturgy of life. We live out of the paschal mystery, seeking to do all we can to conform our thoughts, words, and actions to the mind of Christ. In this final chapter, we will examine precisely what it means for Christians to live out of the paschal mystery. We will do so by offering a concrete way of first discerning out of and then acting according to the mystery of Jesus' passion, death, and resurrection. This mystery, the paschal mystery, is meant to shape every aspect of our lives on earth.

Contemplating the Face of Christ

In *Novo millennio ineunte,* his apostolic letter on the church in the new millennium, Pope John Paul II emphasized the importance of prayer for the future of the church, especially contemplative prayer. He bade Christians the world over to contemplate the face of Christ so that the Spirit of Christ might touch and inspire them to follow the way of love.[2]

When we contemplate that face, the false images we have of God gradually break up and lose their hold over us. Jesus dispels our stereotypes and reveals to us the power of the divine in the fullness of his humanity. This happens by means of a mutual, reciprocal gaze. It begins when we open our hearts to him in prayer and become still in his presence. We look into his eyes and allow him to look into ours. We peer into his soul, and he peers into ours. We get to know him, and he gets to know us. In the midst of this stillness, we experience Jesus in the depths of our hearts. We gaze upon his humanity and touch the mystery of his divinity. He, in turn, gazes upon our humanity and sees there the person each of us is destined to become.

Contemplating the face of Christ is the necessary backdrop for living out of the paschal mystery. If we do not gaze into his eyes and allow him to gaze into ours in a quiet, intimate, prayerful exchange of hearts, we will never know what it means to be his friend. What is more, if we fail to befriend him and allow him to befriend us, we will never understand why he gave up his life for us. Jesus gave himself up for us out of love for us: "There is no greater love than this: to lay down one's life for one's friends" (John 15:13). His paschal mystery is rooted in his deep and sincere desire to become our friend. To live out of the paschal mystery is to live in friendship with Christ. That friendship is based not on utility or pleasure, but on goodness and truth. It is benevolent and reciprocal, and it results in a mutual indwelling.[3] We dwell in Jesus' heart, and Jesus, through the pouring out of his Spirit, dwells in ours. St. Alphonsus de Liguori, the patron saint of confessors and moral theologians, puts it very eloquently: "Paradise for God ... is the human heart."[4] Jesus' paschal mystery is an expression of his deep desire to dwell in our hearts as the crucified and risen Lord. He died for that reason, and he rose from the dead for that reason. We can adapt St. Alphonsus's words slightly to highlight an important truth for us: Heaven for us is to dwell in the heart of Christ. We dwell in Christ's heart by turning to him in prayer, by contemplating his face, and most especially by receiving him in the Eucharist.

Dwelling in Christ's Heart

According to J. B. Phillips, in Jesus Christ "God 'focused' in humanity, speaking a language, expressing thoughts, and demonstrating life in terms that [we] can understand."[5] As a result, humanity was given the opportunity to see God "not seated on a high throne, but down in the battlefield of life."[6] From Jesus, we learn to call God "Abba, Father." We also learn that the purpose of life is to love God with all our hearts and to love others as we love ourselves. Sin, according to Phillips, lies in the refusal to follow this simple mandate.[7] Those who follow these principles lead lives centered not on the self, but on Christ. Phillips contrasts the different mind-sets of those who dwell in Christ's heart and those who do not.

Most people think:
Happy are the pushers, for they get on in the world.
Happy are the hard-boiled, for they never let life hurt them.
Happy are they who complain, for they get their own way in the end.
Happy are the blasé, for they never worry over their sins.
Happy are the slave-drivers, for they get results.
Happy are the knowledgeable men of the world, for they know their way around.
Happy are the trouble-makers, for people have to take notice of them.

Jesus Christ said:
Happy are those who realize their spiritual poverty; they have already entered the kingdom of Reality.
Happy are they who bear their share of the world's pain; in the long run they will know more happiness than those who avoid it.

> Happy are those who accept life and their own limitations;
> they will find more in life than anybody.
> Happy are those who long to be truly "good"; they will fully
> realize their ambition.
> Happy are those who are ready to make allowances and to
> forgive; they will know the love of God.
> Happy are those who are real in their thoughts and feelings;
> in the end they will see the ultimate Reality, God.
> Happy are those who help others to live together; they will
> be known to be doing God's work.[8]

Phillips maintains that the poetic form and outdated language of the Beatitudes prevents us from seeing their true revolutionary character. Jesus came into this world to revolutionize the hearts of his followers. We find happiness (beatitude, heaven) by dwelling in his heart and by allowing his Spirit to dwell in ours. We do this not through our own efforts, but by humbly coming to the Lord and inviting him into our hearts.

When we look at the Eucharist, we can take Phillips's insight about God focusing himself in Jesus one step further. In Jesus Christ, we have been given an adequate understanding not only of who God is, but also of the kind of people we are called to become. The Eucharist is the most prominent means through which that transformation in our lives takes place. When we receive the Eucharist, our communion with Christ and with one another deepens. The body and blood of Christ enters us and becomes a part of us. God, one might say, uses the Eucharist to focus himself in the community of believers. Through this sacrament, Jesus' paschal mystery unfolds before us and enters our very lives. The Eucharist is the source and summit of our lives because, through it, our friendship with Christ is nourished and sustained. In other words, God focuses himself in Jesus and, through the Eucharist, in the community of believers as well. Through this "sacrament of thanksgiving," we embrace the call to discipleship and seek to share with others the friendship that has transformed our lives. Like Christ, we do so by (1) entering the worlds of those around us (as in the incarnation), (2) giving of ourselves to them completely (as in Jesus' ministry, passion, and death), so that (3) we can become nourishment for them (as in the Eucharist), and (4) a source of hope (as in the resurrection and ascension). This fourfold movement demonstrates the meaning of Christ's love for us and gives us a concrete way of discerning and living out the meaning of the paschal mystery in our lives.[9]

Discerning Out of Mystery

If contemplating the face of Christ is the necessary backdrop against which we live out of the paschal mystery, and if a mutual indwelling of hearts describes the process through which we appropriate the revolutionary values of the kingdom, then a question arises about how we can authentically and practically discern out of that mystery in order to make sound, reasoned decisions about the practical spiritual and moral issues that we face on a daily basis. What follows is a concrete way of bringing the insights gained from our investigation of the narrative contours of Christ's paschal mystery into the decision-making process of our everyday lives. This approach represents a set of guidelines that should help Christians reach sound spiritual and moral decisions that closely correspond to the fourfold movement of Christ's life. To highlight the role conversion plays in this process, we will juxtapose on this movement the developmental approach of the three ways that helped us so much in the last chapter to understand the paschal mystery, its relationship to the eucharistic celebration, and its impact on conscience formation.

He Entered Our World

Christ's paschal mystery has its origin in the mystery of his incarnation. The divine *Logos* entered our world and became one of us. Jesus' humanity was real, not a mask. In Jesus, God enters the world of human experience and embraces every dimension of it, being like us in all things, save sin (cf. Heb 4:15). He entered our world so that we might enter his and become like him. This first movement has important meaning for how we live our lives. In our spiritual and moral decision making, we follow in the footsteps of Christ by doing our best to enter the worlds of those around us. Wherever we are— be it at home or at work, in school or at play—the call of discipleship bids us to enter into the circumstances of those around us so that we can understand their needs and enter into solidarity with them. It will be impossible for us to understand what is being asked of us as disciples of Christ in a given situation if we are afraid to step out of our private worlds and to risk reaching out and touching the lives of those in need. Our mission as Christ's disciples is to put our private concerns behind us so that we can espouse gospel values and carry them to far and distant lands. For some, this calling means actually traveling to the farthest ends of the earth. For others, it means exploring the deepest recesses of another's heart by the light of Christ's message. This first step in our method for discerning out of Christ's paschal mystery may be refined by looking at the threefold way of purgation, illumination, and union.

The Purgative Way. Before entering another's world, we must be sure that we are not carrying with us any biases, prejudices, or ideologies that oppose the values of the Beatitudes. To do so, we must examine our hearts and seek to identify the values and principles that truly hold sway over them. Once we have identified any false values and principles, we need to root them out of our lives and take proper precautions so that they will not affect the decision-making process. We can do so in any number of ways: through prayer and fasting, through spiritual direction or conversations with a close friend, through a retreat based on the spiritual exercises, and/or through reception of the sacraments, especially the sacraments of reconciliation and the Eucharist. The most important factor in this point of the process is to be sure that we seek help from God and from those we consider wiser than ourselves.

The Illuminative Way. Once we have tried to identify those values in our lives that run contrary to the gospel, our attempt to enter another's world demands that we seek enlightenment. We must try, in other words, to understand the operative values and principles at work in a particular person's life or in the particular spiritual/moral dilemma we are facing. This means studying the general contours of the person or situation with which we are dealing, doing our best to understand that person or situation, and determining whether they are in accord with the gospel message as it has been handed down in our faith. In making these judgments, it will be important to have access to relevant materials from the world of the particular person or situation we are trying to understand and to compare it with relevant material from the Christian tradition. For Catholics, special attention should be given to the Word of God and the teaching of the magisterium.

The Unitive Way. When Jesus entered our world, he brought with him the love of the Father and the values of the kingdom flowing from that love. In a similar manner, when we seek to enter another's world, we seek to enter into communion with it on the basis of the love that has been revealed to us in Christ. True solidarity with another comes by facing the issues and by entering into a genuine discussion of those issues in the light of the truth of the gospel. The unitive way at this stage of our discernment out of Christ's paschal mystery means sowing the seeds of the good news in another's world so that it might find fertile ground, take root, and grow. The success of our sowing will vary from one context to the next. For it to succeed, we must be willing to enter into dialogue that "is the new name of charity, especially charity within the Church."[10]

Our goal here is for the gospel to take root in a person's life or in a particular situation. However, we do not wish to do so by imposing it on those not yet willing to accept it. Our role is simply to sow the seeds of Christ's love. The Spirit blows where it wills and will forge those bonds of union needed before we can enter the next stage in our process of discernment (cf. John 3:8).

He Gave Himself to Us Completely

Jesus did not merely enter our world; he also gave himself to us completely, to the point of dying on the cross for us. When we think of this outpouring of self, we look to his public ministry of teaching and healing and to the culmination of his love for humanity as manifested in his passion and death. When we seek to discern out of the paschal mystery, it is important that we understand what Christ is asking of us. Like him, we too are called not merely to enter the worlds of those around us, but to give ourselves to them completely. Our response to those in need must be total, not weak and halfhearted. At the same time, we must recognize the limitations within which we must act. Jesus, we must remember, was both God and man. We, on the other hand, are very weak and frail human beings. Our human situation prevents us from giving of ourselves to everyone we meet with the same level of intensity as Jesus did. If we tried to, we would soon be overwhelmed by the constant demands placed upon us and possibly suffer burnout. As Jesus' disciples, we are called to be teachers by word and example. We are also called to be healers of maladies of the human heart. At this stage in our process of discerning out of Christ's paschal mystery, it is essential that we ask the Lord to show us the ones he is asking us to give of ourselves to in this way. We must seek his guidance in trying to understand how he envisions for us our living out of his passion and death. Jesus' paschal mystery continues to this day through our efforts. In seeking that guidance, the threefold way of purgation, illumination, and union once again holds the key to our spiritual/moral discernment.

The Purgative Way. When we look at our call to discipleship in any given situation, it is essential that we take into account our vocational responsibilities and set our priorities straight with them in mind. All disciples seek to follow the way of the Lord Jesus in their lives. Just what that means, however, will differ for an individual or a group, depending on their chosen vocational state in the church. For instance, since a husband's first responsibilities are to his wife and children, he has to be careful not to overload his schedule with added activities (even apostolic ones) that will draw him away from them for extended periods of time and possibly lessen his effectiveness as a husband and a father. In this context, the purgative way requires us to take a good hard look at our lives and to prioritize our responsibilities in such a way that we are living out our chosen vocations firmly rooted in the way of the Lord Jesus. The call to discipleship opens up a variety of paths (e.g., the priesthood, the religious life, married, and single life). Each of us, however, has been called by Jesus to follow a unique path. At this stage of the discernment process, we must recognize that it is impossible for us to follow every possible path. Our concern must be with the particular one that Jesus wants us to walk and to serve those we meet on it with all our hearts.

The Illuminative Way. When giving ourselves to others, it is also important that we take time to figure out the best way for us to do so. Rather than reaching a decision in haste or choosing a course of action without examining all of the possibilities, it is important for us to examine the needs of the situation, prioritize them, and find solutions to them that are consistent with gospel values. As followers of Christ, we are called to foster this reflective attitude toward the people we are called to serve and their various needs. If we wish to give ourselves to others, it is very important that we find a way of giving that will respond to their genuine needs and truly be of help to them. The illuminative way in this process of self-giving underscores the importance of reflecting on gospel values in the context of the concrete circumstances of those concerned. When dealing with important spiritual/moral decisions, we should reflect upon the needs of those concerned in the context of the two most fundamental principles of Jesus' gospel message: loving God with all our hearts and loving our neighbors as ourselves. The close connection between these two principles should help us to look at the people and circumstances we are facing through the eyes of Christ. The question foremost on our minds at all times should be: "What is the most loving thing I can do in the present circumstances?"

The Unitive Way. Giving of ourselves to others involves not only being faithful to our vocational responsibilities and reflecting upon the most loving way to respond to the needs of the moment, but also implementing the insights we have received and carrying out our moral decisions. To give of ourselves requires not only reflection and forethought, but also the concrete implementation of our practical decisions. These should be done for the purpose of bringing those we serve into a deeper union with the love of God. The paschal mystery teaches us that Jesus acts in the world today through the members of his body. Jesus gives of himself through our prudent and thoughtful acts of compassionate love. The unitive way of self-giving reminds us that the goal of our acts of love is union with Christ. We give of ourselves to others because we want them to contemplate the face of Christ and to discern the meaning of their lives out of the depths of his paschal mystery. We act out of union with Christ in order to bring others into union with him. When we face particular spiritual/moral issues in the area of self-giving, we should be asking ourselves what course of action will bring us and the people we serve into closer union with Christ. The values of the kingdom manifested in Jesus' Beatitudes need to be not merely pondered but actually applied to the situation at hand. To be blessed, to be happy, to live in Christ's kingdom is to be in union with God. Union with God is a reflection of one's love of both God and neighbor. As Christ's disciples, we give of ourselves completely in order to make this love present in the here and now. Only in this way will those we serve find union with God and the happiness for which they so desperately search.

He Became Our Food and Source of Nourishment

Jesus not only entered our world and gave of himself completely, but he also became nourishment for us. In the Eucharist, we eat and drink of his body and blood: "For my flesh is real food and my blood real drink" (John 3:8). Jesus' Last Supper with his disciples was intimately connected to his passion, death, and resurrection. When we participate in the eucharistic celebration, we ourselves become more deeply immersed in Christ's paschal mystery and proclaim that we too wish to become nourishment for others. Jesus' offering of his body and blood on the cross is made present in the eucharistic sacrifice and sustains all who partake of it. In a similar way, our offering of self to others is meant to bring spiritual sustenance to those we serve. As disciples, we are called to bring Christ to others and to nourish and sustain their relationship with God. We need food and drink both to sustain ourselves and to give ourselves to others. For this reason, the Eucharist is a sacrament of life and lies at the heart of the efforts of Christ's body to promote life. As disciples of Christ, we are called to promote a "culture of life" in the world.[11] Our giving of self to others is meant to promote this culture from beginning to end. To discern and live out of the paschal mystery means that we are constantly looking for courses of action that further life rather than destroy it. The threefold way of purgation, illumination, and union can help us to understand what it means to be nourishment for others and to stand firmly and resolutely on the side of life.

The Purgative Way. If we truly want our actions to become nourishment for others, we must be willing to look at our own lives and determine which ways of thinking and habits of action promote life and which detract from it. We cannot become nourishment for others if we ourselves refuse to be nourished by Christ and his body, the church. As disciples of Christ, we are called to live *in* the world but not be *of* it. The purgative way of becoming nourishment for others asks us to take a look at the various social and cultural influences on us that poison our outlook on life, our attitudes, and our ways of action. We need to take a thorough inventory of ourselves and do our best to detach ourselves from whatever destructive ways of thinking and acting have made their way into our lifestyle. Our relationship to Christ never remains static: it is moving either along the way of deeper and greater intimacy or away from it. The purgative way at this stage of our discerning and living out of the paschal mystery requires us to be firmly rooted in the way of the Lord Jesus. Jesus himself tells us that we cannot serve two masters (cf. Matt 16:24). As we discern out of the paschal mystery, we must ask ourselves if we are serving the God of life or the god of death. We also need to ask ourselves if our thoughts, words, and actions truly reflect our most deeply held beliefs.

The Illuminative Way. If we wish to become nourishment for others, it is important that we understand what kind of nourishment they need. We are complex creatures with a variety of dimensions in our makeup: the physical, emotional, intellectual, spiritual, and social—to name but a few.[12] In seeking to become nourishment to others, we must try to address those we are serving on every level of their existence. It is difficult to speak to someone on a spiritual level if he or she is suffering from physical hunger and thirst. Similarly, someone may be very intelligent but hurting emotionally and psychologically. To become nourishment for others means that we are willing to bring physical, emotional, intellectual, spiritual, and social food to them. We must do our best to address all of these needs, giving special attention to those needs that are the most neglected and overlooked. The illuminative way of becoming nourishment for others asks us to be conscious of the whole person and of his or her intrinsic dignity by virtue of being created in the image and likeness of God. Because we are called to promote life on all levels of human existence, we must take the time to familiarize ourselves with each of these levels, identify which levels are suffering and most in need of sustenance, and then find appropriate means for nourishing them.

The Unitive Way. Our goal in trying to be nourishment for others should always be to promote life, to make people whole, and to help them deepen their relationship with God. When we do so, we become active practitioners of the "spirituality of communion."[13] It is no accident that the reception of the Eucharist is often referred to as "holy communion." Just as Christ's offering of his body and blood effects a deep, mystical communion between him and his body, the church—giving us access to the communion of love shared by the Father, Son, and Holy Spirit—so too our offering of self creates bonds of solidarity that invite others to share in the bonds of fellowship that make the Christian community a living witness of God's loving presence in the world. The Eucharist is not only a sacrament of life, but also a sacrament of unity. Similarly, in our efforts to become nourishment for others, we seek to be Eucharist to them. That is to say that we try to bear the presence of Christ in their midst and to nourish them with the bonds of authentic Christian friendship. The eucharistic action, in other words, does not end with the last words of the priest at the end of Mass, but continues in our lives as we seek to follow in the footsteps of the Lord by forming ever deeper bonds of communion with the people we are called to serve.

He Became a Source of Hope for Us

Through his resurrection from the dead and ascension into heaven, Jesus became a source of hope for all of humanity. His conquering of death touches one of the deepest aspirations of the human heart. If Jesus gave himself to us completely to the point of dying for us, the empty tomb of Easter morning reminds us that God's love is stronger than death. Through baptism, we become members of Christ's body and are incorporated into his passion, death, and resurrection. For this reason, we too are called to be a source of hope for others. We are called to enter the world of those we serve, to give ourselves to them, to offer them nourishment, and, most importantly, to help them to recognize their final destiny. Jesus' resurrection and ascension reminds us that life does not end in death. Through faith, we join Jesus in death and hope to share in his resurrection (cf. John 11:25). By loving others as Jesus loved us, we become a source of hope for them. Through us, they get a glimpse of God's love for them and receive an insight into the true purpose and meaning of life. Through our actions, hope becomes something concrete and tangible for them. Seeing us living in hope, they themselves are inspired to do the same. How do we live in hope? We do so by rooting our lives in the person and message of Jesus Christ, "the way, the truth, and the life" (John 14:5). These words have special significance for the threefold way of purgation, illumination, and union as it is applied to this final stage of our attempt to discern and live out of the paschal mystery.

The Purgative Way. When trying to inspire others to live in hope in a particular situation, the purgative way reminds us that Jesus himself is "the way." The path of Christian discipleship lies not in the strict and unquestioning adherence to a set of teachings and principles renowned by the Christian faith, but in a deep attachment to the person of Jesus Christ. When trying to find our way through the difficult decisions we must face in life, it is our deep, personal relationship with Christ that will see us through—that and nothing else. Living in hope means that we look at the teaching and principles of our spiritual/moral tradition not as ends in themselves, but as means that others have devised (and, down through the centuries, even revised) to deepen their relationship with the Lord. There is a spiritual dimension to every ethical principle—and vice versa. Living in hope means looking for the voice of the Spirit in the midst of the spiritual and moral dilemmas we face. It means looking at the spiritual/moral predicaments in our lives as part of the warp and woof of our journey to God. Part of the reason people lose hope in certain situations is that they lose sight of the bigger picture of what their decisions mean in terms of their relationship with God and to their final destiny. When we live in hope and seek to help others do the same, we need to take off the spiritual blinders that prevent us from seeing life as Christ would see it and from responding to the circumstances at hand as the Spirit would lead and prompt us. Living in hope means letting go and letting God help us in our attempt to discern and live out of the paschal mystery.

The Illuminative Way. When trying to inspire others to live in hope in a particular situation, the illuminative way reminds us that Jesus is "the truth." Our spiritual/moral decisions are meant to be made in the light of the truth of Jesus Christ. Because of our friendship with Christ, we have been made the adopted sons and daughters of the Father. Because of this divine adoption, we have access to and share in the intimate life of the Trinity—Father, Son, and Spirit. This life is not something removed from our experience, but the most important reality in our lives lying deep within our hearts. To live in hope means to allow the light of Christ to shine within our hearts so that we might discover the Spirit's yearnings deep within us. It means allowing the Spirit to reveal its gifts to us and then our being willing to actually use and apply them in the concrete circumstances of our lives. Many of us simply do not avail ourselves of the gifts the Spirit has given us. Someone who lives in hope is wise, understanding, consulting, knowledgeable, courageous, devout, and awestruck by the majesty of God. These gifts of the Spirit stand at the summit of the spiritual/moral life. They are given to all who share in Christ's

Spirit and are explicitly meant to be used in the circumstances of daily life. To live in hope is to be aware of these gifts at our disposal and to ask the Spirit's guidance in using them prudently and justly.

The Unitive Way. Finally, when trying to inspire others to live in hope in a particular situation, the unitive way reminds us that Jesus is "the life." Jesus is our source of hope because he has risen from the dead and ascended to the Father. His journey through life ends where it began—at the right hand of the Father. Because of the paschal mystery Jesus' life has now become our own. We live in hope because, as members of his body, we believe that our place is with him. This aspect of our discerning and living out of the paschal mystery brings out the eschatological dimension of our spiritual/moral decision making. It reminds us that our decisions have consequences for our lives and that we must remain in Christ if we wish our hope of future glory to become a reality. To be even more concrete, living in hope in this final step of our discernment process means affirming before every person and in every situation we face that Jesus alone is the Lord and master of life. If we call ourselves his disciples, then we cannot compromise on this fundamental premise of our faith. Jesus died on the cross to bring us life in abundance. As his disciples, we take up our cross daily to proclaim his message of abundant life in our particular corner of the world and at our particular moment in time. We do so because Jesus is the world's only hope. Without his person, his mission, and his message, the world would have little cause for hope and nowhere else to turn.

These guidelines for discerning and living out of the paschal mystery are not intended as a method to be applied in a strict, scientific manner to every spiritual/moral dilemma we face, but as a series of insights that should be deeply pondered and used in conjunction with the tried and true principles of the Catholic spiritual/moral tradition. The aim of these guidelines is to help us to look at our spiritual/moral lives in the light of Christ's paschal mystery. When allowed to shine on concrete and practical matters, the light of that mystery helps us to see things in an entirely different way.

Practical Applications

We now want to contemplate how formation within a paschal-mystery consciousness assists in making concrete moral decisions.

Our goal as Christians is to have Christ live his life in us. This goal is achieved through a graced moral development moving us from sin to virtue (that is, the three ways). Within this context we are now ready to ask: "How does this particular act that I am thinking about doing share in the paschal mystery? How does this act incarnate the self-offering hope of Christ himself?" If one discerns that any such act does not share in the paschal mystery or cannot incarnate the mystery of Christ, we have then identified sin. In phrasing the question as we have, we are not reducing Catholic moral living to "acts" per se. We do acknowledge, however, that we solidify our character and determine our orientation to virtue through the thoughtful execution of free acts. A "virtue ethic" is simply an ethic that places the development of character at the center of a person's moral identity. This character, for the Christian, is determined by the capacity of his or her acts to be incorporated into the paschal mystery. The guidelines we are offering are not meant to replace principles of Catholic moral decision making already in place, but to provide the wider context out of which that discernment takes place. We are conscious of the interface not only between any moral issue and our guidelines, but also between our guidelines and the principles that have guided Catholic spiritual reflection in the past (for example, principles of double effect, dignity of the human person, and so forth).

Questions from Personal Morality

Let us imagine that a Catholic is trying to discern if she should join the military as a career....Let us imagine that a judge is deliberating over whether to impose the death sentence on a particular murderer....Let us imagine that a father is deliberating whether to pursue the next degree of career success or stay at home and care for his children....In all of these questions and a thousand others like them, we have to decide which route more fully aligns us to the way of discipleship.

Except for those activities that the Church has recognized as always morally wrong (for example, the taking of innocent human life), most of our decisions come down to a judgment of conscience, as it has been formed by the practice of virtue and influenced by our formative spiritual and intellectual attitudes of mind.[14] Most people do not go through elaborate steps of following delineated methodologies for moral decision making; they simply follow a couple of simple steps. They rest with a felt sense regarding the question. They internalize the pros and cons. They may seek advice from one or two people they trust so that they can hear their decision in the context of another's experience and identity. Some may take the decision to actual prayer. The process does not usually last that long because Americans, at least, feel uncomfortable in a state of abeyance and soon seek a resolution.

The key, then, for contemporary moral decision making is not knowledge of moral methodology. Rather, the weight of decision making falls upon the practices of daily living that make up our religious identity. The crucial component to ethical judgment, then, is connatural knowledge. This is a knowledge that is grasped within as the fruit of many attempts to act and think ethically within the daily practices of one's vocation as Christian. "Aquinas recognizes that the Christian believer can regard the moral life from a double perspective. On the one hand, a person can learn about the Christian moral life from moral argument; on the other hand, the Christian can seize moral truth from personal experience. Aquinas describes this second mode of knowing as the way of connaturality."[15] This connatural knowledge is always to be seen within the context of the virtuous life as completed and crowned by a life lived in the gifts of the Holy Spirit.

Besides this connatural knowledge, it would seem that some type of ad hoc spiritual direction is also needed for a minimum of time, one or two visits. Some might acquaint themselves with church teaching on certain subjects through adult education processes. What appears most universal, however, is what we explored in this book: a Catholic's exposure to the paschal mystery through the liturgy. It is the pattern of the paschal mystery that founds the connatural knowledge of worshipping Catholics. It is this pattern of Christic mystery that truly makes up the conscience of the committed Catholic, even if it has to be awakened or strengthened. It is a foundation configured to the pattern known in the incarnation and the nourishing self-gift of Christ to others, yielding hope in them. This pattern, however, needs to be acknowledged and highlighted through homilies and catechesis for its true impact to take root within the people of the parish. We need to make the content of our moral decision making *conscious,* so it can be publicly presented and argued. In what ways does this pattern form the conscience for concrete judgments in such cases as mentioned above?

All moral decisions are personal: My conscience must be claimed by truth in this particular decision. One's decision, therefore, becomes an incarnation of truth as one knows it. This is not to say that the judgment of conscience is infallible; it simply means that, when the mind is claimed by truth, it is obliged to follow it into action. The previous chapters have made it clear that, for the Christian, the mind that is claimed by moral truth ought to be filled with the reality of the paschal mystery as it is encountered in the eucharistic liturgy. The self-offering of Christ to the Father establishes the pattern of self-offering within our own ego, and thus we defer to the new divine life that seeks to inhabit the mind. For the Christian there really is a core moral question: Can I appropriate the moral truth from within the conscience in and through the power of Christ living his mystery in me?

We strive, therefore, to have our intelligence informed not simply by secular ideas and current opinions but by the person who is Truth, the Christ. The intelligence needs to be fed by the eucharistic action of Christ as he presents himself in word and sacrament. This nourishment for the intellect is amplified in other sources as well, such as theology, philosophy, and all media that bears the truth. The Catholic moral life, therefore, involves two movements: the first is being fed by the substance of virtue, the Christ, and the second is giving nourishment to others by way of our faithful witness. The witness is vital because it establishes moral truth in culture. Secular sources in culture can also bear truth and challenge the conscience to detect it in a process of discernment. What is key for the *faithful* execution of a Christian moral act is the *habitus* that pervades the agent's life. Christ living his life in us is not a phrase of piety yielding warm feelings of closeness to the Christ; it expresses the need for conscience to have a formational context worthy of its mission to judge the truth. The life of immersion in the mysteries of Christ is such a context and yields a life of moral virtue and prudent decision making founded upon and opening up to the call to holiness.

To conclude, the pragmatic questions calling for discernment, such as the examples above, are best approached by placing them in the context of one's vocation and prudently seeking the way that will keep one closer to his or her life's calling (married, single, cleric, religious) from within an ecclesial context aiming the mind, will, and affect toward union with Christ.

Our approach to moral discernment includes the following pastoral realities:

1. The foundation of Christian moral activity and thinking is to be built upon one's entry into the paschal mystery of Christ.

2. This entry occurs through participation in the worship of God the Father at the eucharistic liturgy and as it is recapitulated daily in the sacramental vocation that persons live.

3. This worship affects the mind and heart by purifying one from sin, illuminating the mind with the truths of scripture, and culminating in sacramental and, ultimately, eschatological communion.

4. From this context the believer forms his or her mind into "the mind of Christ." In so doing, each moral question that arises in the course of a day's duties is placed within the Christic mystery and answered in concert with that mystery's content—the Second Person of the Blessed Trinity taking on human nature to become our food and our hope.

5. No act of such a believer can violate the truth as judged within the conscience and formed by adhering to the ordinary magisterium of the church. Each moral action flows from a share in Christ's own virtues as known in yielding to the mystery of the Eucharist, which makes up the heart of the church.

6. The first step of moral discernment is to enter or reenter the mystery; the last step is to enact what this mystery has taught the conscience. The length of time and content of formation between the first and last steps cannot be universally mandated, as each person comes before God as uniquely cherished and known.

7. The content of formation, however, is not to contradict the truths of Christ's own doctrine in scripture and as it unfolds in the magisterium's articulation of such doctrine throughout history in each epoch. We recognize this principle because no one religious leader can take it upon him- or herself to direct

a member of the church into rebellion. To claim a right to this would mean that the individual leader has some form of omniscience not promised to human beings. The doctrine of the church stands as the best judgment of the church now. We live only in the present, and pastoral leaders are called to teach the *recta ratio* of the church as it is now known. On occasion the role of pastoral speculation and prophetic judgment is legitimate, but it cannot be the norm of pastoral discernment and the formation of consciences. A pastoral minister's struggle with a particular moral doctrine cannot be imposed upon a parishioner as a harbinger of development of doctrine. As Mark Graham has noted in his work on the thought of Josef Fuchs, "We should regard the accumulated moral judgments synthesized in moral norms and tested over long periods of time as correct and indicative of *recta ratio*. There might arise instances in the...future that will reveal defects in certain widely accepted moral norms and render them inapplicable in specific concrete situations, but this possibility *should not* influence one's practical, everyday readiness and willingness to accept received ethical wisdom as valid."[16]

With these guidelines, pastoral leaders coax us into discernment and accompany us through to the end as it manifests itself in a particular judgment of conscience. To send discerning believers back to worship is the essence of moral living from the side of mystery. As we feed off the self-offering love and truth of Christ, our conscience becomes hospitable to the judgment of such a worshipping mind.

Concluding Remarks

With Christ we enter into the moral struggles of others through compassion. The church stands ready to assist those who seek moral truth. This assistance comes out of the vast depth of the church's meditation upon and participation in the mystery of Christ's way of life. With each person who comes forward seeking an answer to a moral problem, the church can respond with the hope that such an answer can be found since God's providence extends to the functions of faith-informed reason. Sometimes the truth will be welcomed in joy, at other times such truth will be seen as a cross to bear. No matter the reception given to moral truth by such seekers, the church needs to stand with the one who desires to abide by the judgment of conscience...celebrating with them, or bearing them up under the weight of the cross.

The person who wishes to live a life of virtue is invited to enter the world of Christ and give him- or herself completely over to him. In this way, such a person receives the nourishment and hope that will sustain him or her in living out the transition from vice to virtue. Those who minister the presence of Christ are also asked to take the same journey into the paschal mystery so that they may be sustained in teaching moral truth and in carrying believers through to the peace known from living a holy life (1 Thess 5:23). We could say that this whole book has been about the real gift sent by God in Christ of enabling human beings to share in the divine holiness. At the core of God is holiness, a moral character, as it were, continually flowing over in love and purity. It is the dignity of humans to participate in this divine character, making it now and always true to say that the only tragedy in life is to not be a saint.[17]

Conclusion

> People enter into the highest form of knowledge of God not
> as disparate souls searching their private feelings for clues to
> the nature of God. Rather, the believing community comes to
> know God precisely by being baptismally recreated and
> eucharistically re-membered as the Body of Christ. This is
> not an isolated liturgical event but a daily struggle sacra-
> mentalized in the liturgy; it is the discovery of personhood in
> living out the concrete manifestations of the paschal mystery
> in the daily details of one's existence.
>
> Mark McIntosh
> *Mystical Theology*[1]

In this book we have explored what it means to live out "the concrete
manifestations of the paschal mystery in the daily details of one's
existence." We focused particularly on the formation of conscience
within the eucharistic liturgy, the ways of spiritual progress that
make up the core of moral conversion, and the need for discernment
of actions. Our effort has been to place all these concerns of moral
living within the apex of Christian reality, the paschal mystery. In
order to create a moral theology more suited to the development of
virtue and Christian practice, one has to locate the core of such a
theology within the truth of Christ's own self-giving to the Father "for
us and for our salvation." To think out of this context is truly the
unique contribution of Christian ethics to the world.

Theologian John Dunne has written that a person has to discover a life that can live on through death.[2] We believe that such a
life is found in two ways: clinging to the knowledge of truth as conscience presents it, and clinging to love in the eucharistic mystery. To
do this yields a knowing that comes from loving. Only when one
actually enters into the mystery of Christ's self-offered life can sin be
healed. It is the mystery that heals: not the law, not ritual, not ther-

apy, not education, but the mystery of Christ. For those serious about taking on the discipline of a moral conversion, entering the paschal mystery presents itself as the supreme way to happiness.

In writing this book we wanted to probe an approach to moral reflection and living that highlights the spiritual, symbolic, and sacramental realities of faith. The symbol of Christ among us, as our savior who gave his life so that humans might find their way back to the Father, inspires today as it did two thousand years ago. Such a symbol of love moves the sinner to repent and become vulnerable to the truths of such divine love working upon the operations of the mind in its search for truth and meaning. It may be true that the ethical mandate of Christ, in the parable of the Good Samaritan, is for his followers to "go and do likewise" (Luke 10:37), but we will never be able to choose the welfare of others over our own unless we have internalized our love for God and live out of the power of his indwelling presence.

The harnessing of this divine power living within us enables us to choose the good despite the often unpleasant effects upon the self. The reception of holy communion, as the culmination of being present to God and God's presence to us in the eucharistic liturgy, establishes this indwelling and embeds it within each member of the church. Participation in the paschal mystery through the symbols of the eucharistic liturgy is not simply a devotion or piety but the very lifeblood of all Christians who would seek to know and do what is good in the eyes of Christ. For theologians and pastoral ministers to move these symbols to the core of moral formation, teaching, and living would unlock a dynamic source from which the conscience and the moral imagination can be fed.

The goal of such moral formation is not to produce an astonishing moral person, someone singular and odd, but, rather, an original copy of the Christ. This is what sainthood is all about, a life that emits an attraction that leads others only to the Christ who dwells within the saint and not to the saint him- or herself. We would hope that highlighting the symbol of the paschal mystery in moral formation will lead others to further reflect upon its powerful influence in the development of Christian virtue, conscience, and holiness.

Notes

Chapter One

1. For both quotations, see *Catechism of the Catholic the Church* (Vatican City: Libreria Editrice Vaticana, 1994), no. 571.

2. For the biblical roots of the terms, see *The New Dictionary of Theology*, eds, Joseph A. Komonchak, Mary Collins, and Dermot A. Lane (Dublin: Gill and Macmillan, 1987), s.v. "Paschal Mystery," by James L. Empereur.

3. Cyprian Vagaggini, *Theological Dimensions of the Liturgy: A General Treatise on the Theology of the Liturgy*, trans. Leonard J. Doyle and W. A. Jurgens (Collegeville, MN: The Liturgical Press, 1976), 252.

4. Thomas Aquinas distinguishes the redemption of fallen humanity in terms of a twofold movement of healing (i.e., from the effects of original sin) and elevation (i.e., to participate in the divine nature). See *Summa theologiae* I–II, q. 109, a. 2, resp.; a. 4, resp. The second element of this movement of redemptive grace (that of "elevation") corresponds exactly to the concept of "divinization" developed by the Greek fathers.

5. In Catholic teaching, the positive universal constants of human experience have traditionally been identified with the doctrine of Creation; the negative, with effects of original sin. See *The Catechism of the Catholic Church*, nos. 356–61, 405. See also Thomas Aquinas, *Summa theologiae*, I, q. 93, aa. 1–9; I–II, q. 85, a. 3, resp.; Ludwig Ott, *The Fundamentals of Catholic Dogma*, trans. Patrick Lynch (Rockford, IL: Tan Books, 1974), 94–100, 113.

6. For a treatment of Jesus and the universal *humanum,* see Edward Schillebeeckx, *Jesus: An Experimental Christology* (New York: Crossroad, 1985), 602–12. See also Idem, *Christ: The Experience of Jesus as Lord* (New York: Crossroad, 1981), 734–43.

7. For the admission of four gospels rather than one into the New Testament, see Raymond E. Brown, *An Introduction to the New Testament* (New York: Doubleday, 1997), 12–15. See also Raymond E. Brown and Raymond F. Collins, "Canonicity," in *The New Jerome*

Biblical Commentary, eds. Raymond E. Brown, Joseph A. Fitzmyer, and Roland E. Murphy (London: Geoffrey Chapman, 1989), 1046–47.

8. See above n. 1.

9. For Christ as the language of God, see Hans Urs von Balthasar, *A Theological Anthropology* (New York: Sheed and Ward, 1967), 275–305.

10. For the central position of the paschal mystery in the plan of salvation, see Vagaggini, *Theological Dimensions of the Liturgy,* 250.

11. This section presents in modified form material first developed in Dennis J. Billy, *Evangelical Kernels: A Theological Spirituality of the Religious Life* (Staten Island, NY: Alba House, 1993), 95–108. See also Idem, "The Redemption Kernel," *Review for Religious* 49 (1990): 256–64.

12. For the concept of ransom in the Jewish scriptures in early Christianity, see Frances M. Young, *Sacrifice and the Death of Christ,* with a Foreword by Maurice Wiles (Philadelphia: The Westminster Press, 1975), 36, 57, 67, 78, 80. For Aquinas's refinement of Anselm's satisfaction model, see *Summa theologiae,* III, q. 1, a. 2, resp.; III, q. 46, aa. 1–3. For Luther's understanding of redemption, see Gustaf Aulén, *Christus Victor: An Historical Study of the Three Main Types of the Idea of the Atonement,* trans. A. G. Herbert (New York: Macmillan, 1969), 101–22. For a description of early Catholic suspicions of subjective atonement (i.e., Bernard of Clairvaux vs. Abelard), see J. Rivière, *Le dogme de la redemption,* 2d ed. (Paris: Librairie Victor Lecoffre, 1905), 333–442. For the guarded reaction of the magisterium toward liberation theology, see The Sacred Congregation for the Doctrine of the Faith, "Instruction on Certain Aspects of the 'Theology of Liberation'" in *Liberation Theology: A Documentary History,* ed. Alfred T. Hennelly (Maryknoll, NY: Orbis Books, 1990), 393–414; Idem, "Instruction on Christian Freedom and Liberation," in *Liberation Theology,* 461–97.

13. See Athanasius, *De incarnatione,* 54.3 (*Sources chrétiennes,* 199:458–59; *Patrologia graeca,* 25:191–92).

14. In this respect, the development of doctrine is not a linear historical progression, where one theological model emerges from and incorporates previous formulations, but an interlocking web of penetrating insights into the nature of a mystery that no single historically conditioned linguistic formulation can ever exhaust.

15. The doctrine of Trinitarian perichoresis *(circumincessio)* asserts both the penetration and mutual indwelling of the Father, Son, and Spirit and the essential unity of their *ad extra* activities. For the

unity of the immanent Trinity and economic Trinity, see Walter Kasper, *The God of Jesus Christ* (New York: Crossroad, 1984), 273–77.

16. *"Bonum diffusivum sui"* ("The good is self-diffusive"). This medieval Latin phrase has become axiomatic in describing the love of the Trinity. It has its origins in the sixth-century Neoplatonic writings of Pseudo-Dionysius the Areopagite, *De divinibus nominibus*, 4.1, 4.2, 4.20 (*Patrologia graeca*, 3:693–96, 717–22).

17. In the words of Alphonsus de Liguori, "It was not necessary for the Redeemer to die in order to save the world; a drop of his blood, a single tear, or prayer, was sufficient to procure salvation for all; for such a prayer, being of infinite value, should be sufficient to save not one but a thousand worlds." See *Dignity and Duties of the Priest, or Selva*, vol. 12, *The Complete Ascetical Works of St. Alphonsus de Liguori*, ed. Eugene Grimm (Brooklyn: Redemptorist Fathers, 1927), 26. According to Thomas Aquinas, God could have redeemed humanity in many other ways, but becoming man and dying on the cross were the most appropriate for healing the wretchedness of the human condition, see *Summa theologiae*, III, q. 1, a. 1, resp.

18. For example, the ransom, satisfaction, and subjective atonement theories of redemption all place the cross at the center of the redemptive mystery with the resurrection being merely ancillary. See Aulén, *Christus Victor*, 143–59. For Jesus' resurrection as a redemptive event, see Walter Kasper, *Jesus the Christ* (London/New York: Burns & Oates/Paulist Press, 1976), 154–60.

19. See, for example, the theology of the paschal mystery presented in Dermot A. Lane, *Christ at the Centre: Selected Issues in Christology* (New York/Mahwah, NJ: Paulist Press, 1991), 103–29.

20. See above n. 13.

21. Horace Bushnell, *The Vicarious Sacrifice* (1866). Cited in Kenneth Leech, *Experiencing God: Theology as Spirituality* (New York: Harper and Row, 1985), 301.

22. See Vagaggini, *Theological Dimensions of the Liturgy*, 270.

23. See *The New Dictionary of Theology*, s.v. "Paschal Mystery," by James L. Empereur.

24. For these and other analogous uses of the term *sacrament*, see Michael Schmaus, *Dogma*, vol. 5, *The Church as Sacrament* (London: Sheed and Ward, 1975), 1–19. For more detailed studies, see Edward Schillebeeckx, *Christ the Sacrament of the Encounter with God*, with a foreword by Cornelius Ernst (New York: Sheed and Ward, 1963) and Colman E. O'Neill, *Meeting Christ in the Sacraments*, revised ed., Romanus Cessario (New York: Alba House, 1991). See also *The Catechism of the Catholic Church*, nos. 1113–1130.

25. For how the Latin term *sacramentum* came to be a synonym for the Greek term *mysterion*, see Vagaggini, *Theological Dimensions of the Liturgy*, 605–6.

26. John Navone and Thomas Cooper, *Tellers of the Word* (New York: Le Jacq Publishing, 1981), 269.

27. For a treatment of these marks of friendship and their relevance to our friendship with Christ, see Paul J. Wadell, *Friendship and the Moral Life* (Notre Dame, IN: University of Notre Dame Press, 1989), 130–41.

28. See John Paul II, *Evangelium vitae*, no. 28.

29. Ibid.

30. The addition of *lex agendi* to the theological principle *lex orandi, lex credendi* comes from Don. E. Saliers. See E. Byron Anderson and Bruce T. Morrill, eds., *Liturgy and the Moral Self: Humanity at Full Stretch before God* (Collegeville, MN: The Liturgical Press, 1998), 4–8.

31. See Peter Brown, *The Making of Late Antiquity* (Cambridge, MA: Harvard University Press, 1978), 54–80.

32. See, for example, *De civitate Dei*, 13.14 in *Corpus Christianorum Series Latina*, 48:395–96. For the development of Augustine's concept of "seminal nature," see Gabriel Daly, "Theological Models in the Doctrine of Original Sin," *The Heythrop Journal* 13 (1972): 121–42.

33. For examples, see Daly, "Theological Models in the Doctrine of Original Sin," 138–40.

34. See John Paul II, *Novo millennio ineunte*, no. 43.

35. Alphonsus de Liguori, *The Way of Conversing Always and Familiarly with God*, vol. 2, *The Complete Ascetical Works of St. Alphonsus de Liguori*, 395.

Chapter Two

1. J. N. D. Kelly, *Early Christian Creeds*, 3d ed. (New York: Longman, 1972), 297–98.

2. See John Paul II, *Ecclesia de Eucharistia*, no. 3.

3. Vagaggini, *Theological Dimensions of the Liturgy*, 250.

4. Second Vatican Council, *Sacrosanctum concilium*, no. 7, in Walter M. Abbott, SJ, and Joseph Gallagher, SJ, eds., *The Documents of Vatican II* (New York: The America Press, 1966), 140–41.

5. Ibid., 141.

6. Second Vatican Council, *Lumen gentium*, no. 11, in *The Documents of Vatican II*, 28; Idem, *Presbyterorum ordinis*, no. 5, in *The Documents of Vatican II*, 541.

7. This section and the one that follows present in modified form insights first presented in Billy, *Evangelical Kernels*, 135–50. See

also Dennis J. Billy, "The Bread Kernel," *Review for Religious* 50 (1991): 749–58.

8. For those passages in John's Gospel that, according to the standards of the historical critical method, may be considered acceptable or, at least, possible allusions to the Eucharist, see Raymond E. Brown, *New Testament Essays* (New York: Paulist Press, 1965), 76.

9. In this respect, the gospels preserve not only Jesus' authentic words of institution, but also theological reflection upon them by early Christian communities in light of his entire life.

10. For the nature of prophetic symbolism, see Raymond E. Brown, Joseph A. Fitzmyer, and Roland E. Murphy, eds., *The Jerome Biblical Commentary*, vol. 1, *The Old Testament* (Englewood Cliffs, NJ: Prentice-Hall, 1968), s.v. "Introduction to Prophetic Literature," by Bruce Vawter.

11. Of the three, the second (i.e., the eucharistic presence) is the most difficult to establish in early Christian sources. In the words of Jaroslav Pelikan: "The theologians did not have adequate concepts within which to formulate a doctrine of the real presence that evidently was already believed by the church even though it was not yet taught by explicit instruction or confessed by creeds." See his *The Christian Tradition: A History of The Development of Doctrine*, vol. 1, *The Emergence of the Christian Tradition* (100–600) (Chicago: University of Chicago Press, 1971), 168. For one of the clearest assertions in early Christian literature of Christ's real eucharistic presence, see Ignatius of Antioch, *Letter to the Smyrnaeans*, 7.1 in *Apostolic Fathers I*, The Loeb Classical Library (Cambridge, MA/London: Harvard University Press/ William Heinemann LTD, 1977), 274–75 (*Patrologia graeca*, 5:713–14).

12. See John Paul II, *Ecclesia de Eucharistia*, no. 61.

13. For the eschatological context of the church's eucharistic banquet, see Vatican Council II, *Lumen gentium*, no. 48 in Norman P. Tanner, ed., *Decrees of the Ecumenical Councils*, vol. 2 (London/ Washington, DC: Sheed and Ward/Georgetown University Press, 1990), 887–88. See also Schmaus, *The Church as Sacrament*, 134–38; Jean Galot, "Pasto escatologico," *Vita consecrata* 26 (1990): 783–99; John Paul II, *Ecclesia de Eucharistia*, nos. 16–20.

14. For the official magisterial use of the term *transubstantiation*, see H. Denzinger and A. Schönmetzer, eds., *Enchiridion Symbolorum*, 32d ed. (Barcelona: Herder, 1963), nos. 802 [430], 860 [465], 1642 [877]. According to the last reference, from the Council of Trent's "Decree on the Most Holy Eucharist," the conversion of the

bread and wine into the body and blood of Christ is "appropriately and properly" *(conveniter et proprie)* called transubstantion. Since the development of a more precise formulation using different philosophical categories is not specifically addressed, the possibility would seem to remain an open issue for Catholic theology. As recently as 1965, however, Paul VI insisted that terms such as "transignification" (i.e., a change in meaning) and "transfinalization" (i.e., a change in purpose) did not sufficiently explain the real presence. See *Mysterium fidei*, nos. 10–12 in *Acta Apostolicae Sedis* 57 (1965): 755–56; for the English translation, see *The Pope Speaks* 10 (no. 4, 1965): 311–12. For a restatement of the church's teaching on Christ's presence in the Eucharist, see John Paul II, *Ecclesia de Eucharistia*, no. 15.

15. For the various theories of how this takes place, see Ott, *Fundamentals of Catholic Dogma*, 410–12. For recent magisterial teaching on the Eucharist as sacrifice, see John Paul II, *Ecclesia de Eucharistia*, nos. 11–20.

16. While Christians should therefore understand their own participation in Christ's redemptive mission as occurring throughout the whole of their lives, it is affirmed most profoundly when they gather for the eucharistic banquet. In the words of the Second Vatican Council: "As often as the sacrifice of the cross in which 'Christ, our passover, has been sacrificed' (1 Cor 5:7), is celebrated on an altar, the work of our redemption is carried on." See *Lumen gentium*, no. 3 in Abbott, ed., *The Documents of Vatican II*, 16.

17. That is to say, the work of redemption is accomplished in us in a special way through the Eucharist, the participation in and reception of which enables us to manifest the mystery of Christ and his church more clearly. See Vatican Council II, *Sacrocanctum concilium*, no. 2 in Tanner, ed., *Decrees of the Ecumenical Councils*, 2:820. See also F. X. Durrwell, *In the Redeeming Christ: Toward a Theology of Spirituality*, trans. Rosemary Sheed (New York: Sheed and Ward, 1963), 54–63.

18. John Paul II, *Ecclesia de Eucharistia*, no. 5.

19. In this respect, the term *transubstantiation* is an orthodox formulation of the Catholic faith, but does not, in and of itself, exhaust the full meaning of the mystery of Christ's presence in the consecrated eucharistic species. The possibility therefore remains for: (1) other formulations to develop over time and be incorporated into the tradition that will express the mystery more fully and (2) other formulations that will capture certain aspects of the mystery more fully and that can then be used in conjunction with the more traditional

expressions. For present magisterial use of the term, see John Paul II, *Ecclesia de Eucharistia*, no. 15. For a postmodern reading of the term *transubstantiation*, see David Crownfield, "The Seminal Trace: Presence, Difference, and Transubstantiation," *Journal of the American Academy of Religion* 59 (1991): 361–71.

20. For the Eucharist as the source from which all the church's power flows, see Vatican Council II, *Sacrosanctum concilium*, no. 10 in *Decrees of the Ecumenical Councils*, 2:823. See also *Codex iuris canonici*, can. 897 in *Code of Canon Law: Latin-English Edition* (Washington, DC: Canon Law Society of America, 1983), 336–37; John Paul II, *Ecclesia de Eucharistia*, nos. 1–3.

21. It was probably an excessive focus on private eucharistic devotion in popular piety in the period immediately prior to the Second Vatican Council that led to its demise in many sectors of the postconciliar church. In any case, eucharistic devotions, both public and private, are encouraged by the church, provided they follow the norms established by legitimate authority. See Vatican Council II, *Sacrosanctum concilium*, no. 13 in *Decrees of the Ecumenical Councils*, 2:824; the Sacred Congregation of Rites, *Eucharisticum mysterium*, chap. III, part I in *Acta Apostolicae Sedis* 59 (1967): 569; for the English translation, Austin Flannery, gen. ed., *Vatican Council II: The Conciliar and Post Conciliar Documents* (Northport, NY: Costello, 1975), 132. See also John Paul II, *Ecclesia de Eucharistia*, no. 25.

22. For the Eucharist as the sacrament of Christian unity, see Colman O'Neill, *Meeting Christ in the Sacraments*, revised ed., Romanus Cessario, 178–80. See also Vatican Council II, *Unitatis redintegratio*, no. 2 in *Decrees of the Ecumenical Councils*, 2:908–9; John Paul II, *Ecclesia de Eucharistia*, nos. 34–46.

23. See Schmaus, *The Church as Sacrament*, 134–38; Galot, "Pasto eschatologico," 797–99; John Paul II, *Ecclesia de Eucharistia*, nos. 19–20.

24. In this respect, the image in *The Didache* of the broken bread that "…was scattered upon the mountains, but was brought together and became one" (chap. 9) has implications not only for the church as a mystical corporate entity, but also for its ongoing theological reflection. See *Apostolic Fathers I*, Loeb Classical Library, 322–23. On the unity of theology, see Thomas Aquinas, *Summa theologiae*, I, q. 1, a. 3.

25. See chap. 1, n. 30.

26. See *Institutio Generalis Missalis Romani (2000)*, nos. 46–54.

27. The word *parish* comes from the Greek word *paroikia*, meaning "sojourners in a foreign land." It was used by early Christian

communities to remind believers that their true country and citizenship was in heaven (cf. 1 Pet 1:17). For relevant references, see Walter Bauer, "Paroikia," *A Greek-English Lexicon of the New Testament and Other Early Christian Literature*, 2d ed. (revised and augmented from Bauer's 5th edition, 1958), trans. and eds., F. W. Gingrich, F. W. Danker, W. F. Arndt (Chicago/London: University of Chicago Press, 1979), 629.

28. See *Institutio Generalis Missalis Romani (2000)*, nos. 55–71.

29. Ibid., nos. 73–76.

30. Ibid., nos. 77–79.

31. Ibid., nos. 80–89.

32. Ibid., no. 90.

33. Augustine of Hippo, *De civitate Dei*, 14.28 in *Corpus Christianorum Series Latina*, 48:451–52.

34. See chapter 1, n. 13.

Chapter Three

1. Livio Melina, *Sharing in Christ's Virtues* (Washington, DC: The Catholic University of America Press, 2001), 154.

2. James Keating and David McCarthy, "Moral Theology with the Saints," *Modern Theology* 19, no. 2 (April 2003): 203–18.

3. Raniero Cantalamessa, *The Mystery of Easter* (Collegeville, MN: Liturgical Press, 1993), 60.

4. Dom Columba Marmion, *Christ and His Mysteries* (St. Louis, MO: Herder, 1939), 348.

5. Ibid., 349.

6. Brian Johnstone, CSsR, "Resurrection and Moral Theology," *Josephinum Journal of Theology* n.s. 7, nos. 1–2 (2000): 15.

7. Ibid., 11. See also Romans 6:4, 4:25.

8. Catholic Church, Vatican Council II, *Gaudium et Spes* (*The Church in the Modern World*, 1965), no. 22.

Chapter Four

1. Louis Bouyer, *Introduction to Spirituality* (Collegeville, MN: Liturgical Press, 1961), 248.

2. Hugh of Balma, "The Roads to Zion Mourn," in *Carthusian Spirituality*, trans. Dennis Martin, Classics of Western Spirituality Series (Mahwah, NJ: Paulist Press, 1997), 70.

3. Bouyer, *Introduction to Spirituality*, 243–85.

4. Ibid., 245.

5. Ibid., 275.

6. Ibid., 246.

7. Ibid., 247.

8. Ibid., 255.

9. See Servais Pinckaers, *The Pursuit of Happiness God's Way—Living the Beatitudes* (Staten Island, NY: Alba House, 1998).

10. Ibid., 71.

11. John Paul II, *Veritatis Splendor* (*The Splendor of Truth*, 1993), nos. 22 and 103.

12. Jonathan Robinson, *Spiritual Combat Revisited* (San Francisco: Ignatius, 2003), 239–40.

13. Jonathan Robinson, *On the Lord's Appearing* (Washington, DC: The Catholic University of America Press, 1997), 202–3, 213.

14. Saint Augustine, *Confessions* (New York: Image Books, 1960), bk. 10, chap. 27, n. 38.

15. Bouyer, *Introduction to Spirituality*, 264.

16. Ibid., 276.

17. For a good summary of the three ways in the context of other approaches to moral/spiritual development, see Robinson, *On the Lord's Appearing*, 78–84.

18. John Paul II, *Veritatis Splendor,* no. 15. See also nos. 22 and 103.

19. Thomas Merton, *The Seven Storey Mountain* (New York: Harcourt, Brace and Co., 1948), 158, 163.

20. Ibid., 210–11.

21. John Henry Newman, *Parochial and Plain Sermons,* vol. 1 (London: Longmans, Green, and Co., 1900), 11.

22. See James Keating, *Listening for Truth: Praying Our Way to Virtue* (St. Louis, MO: Liguori Publications, 2002).

23. By saying this, we do not discount the graces known in the course of practicing virtue outside of worship. We are simply recognizing that the paschal mystery as sacramentally represented within the Eucharist is the source of all such graces, whether acknowledged or not. Also consult Kathleen Calahan, *Formed in the Image of Christ: The Sacramental-Moral Theology of Bernard Häring* (Collegeville, MN: Liturgical Press, 2004).

24. Columba Marmion, *Christ in His Mysteries,* 10th ed. (St. Louis: Herder, 1939), 353–54.

25. Ibid., 10–16.

26. Ibid., 348.

27. Ibid., 349.

28. "Thus, according to a formula reiterated by a number of Church Fathers, 'God has become man so that man might become God.' And just as the humanity of God is the work of his grace, so also this divinisation of man is the work of Christ's grace. Man does

not become God by nature, 'which is even more foolish than heretical' (4th Lateran Council), but by participation in the divine filiation of Jesus Christ" (Jean Borella, *The Sense of the Supernatural* (Edinburgh: T & T Clark, 1998), 82.

29. See Anthony Draper, *The Understanding of the Christian Life in the Work of Abbot Columba Marmion* (Maynooth, Ireland, 1983), 368.

30. This communal reality can be looked at not only from the perspective of holiness but also from one of sin as well. "The awareness of sin as sin, therefore, only opens fully when we are set in relation to God and in solidarity with others. If one forgets the relational context, the gift of a forgiving relationship with God and the solidarity with one another in the need and desire for forgiveness, any talk of sin rapidly degenerates into forms of...self-centeredness." Ronald Mercier, SJ, "What Are We to Make of Sin? Allison's Challenge to Moral Theology" *Josephinum Journal of Theology* n.s. 10, no. 2 (Summer/Fall 2003): 283.

31. John of the Cross, *Living Flame*, vol. 3, par. 32. See David Knowles, *The Nature of Mysticism* (New York: Hawthorn Books, 1966), 99.

32. Marmion, *Christ in His Mysteries*, 353–54.

33. Dietrich Von Hildebrand, *Transformation in Christ* (Manchester, NH: Sophia, 1990), 232–33.

34. Charles Shelton, *Achieving Moral Health* (New York: Crossroad, 2000), 48.

35. Marmion, *Christ in His Mysteries*, 353.

36. Louis Gillon, OP, *Christ and Moral Theology* (Staten Island, NY: Alba House, 1967), 62–75.

37. See James Keating and David McCarthy, "Habits of Holiness: The Ordering of Moral-Mystical Living," *Communio* 28 (Winter 2001): 820–42.

Chapter Five

1. J. B. Phillips, *Your God Is Too Small* (1961; New York: Macmillan, 1967), 119.

2. John Paul II, *Novo millennio ineunte* (Beginning the New Millennium, January 6, 2001), nos. 16–28.

3. See the description of charity as friendship with God in Thomas Aquinas's *Summa Theologiae* II–II q.23 a.1 resp. For mutual indwelling as a result of friendship, see Idem, *Summa Theologiae* I–II q.28 a.2 resp. See also chap. 1, n.27.

4. Alphonsus de Liguori, *The Way of Conversing Always and Familiarly with God*, vol. 2, *The Complete Ascetical Works of St. Alphonsus de Liguori* (Brooklyn: Redemptorist Fathers, 1926), 395.

5. Phillips, *Your God Is Too Small*, 73–74.

6. Ibid., 74.

7. Ibid., 89–90.

8. Ibid., 92–93 (see Matt 5:3–12; Luke 6:20–26).

9. For an extended treatment of these four christological movements, see Billy, *Evangelical Kernels*, 17–31.

10. This description of "dialogue" appears in John Paul II, *Vita Consecrata* (The Consecrated Life, 1996), no. 74.

11. For the conflict between the "culture of life" and the "culture of death," see John Paul II, *Evangelium Vitae* (On the Value and Inviolability of Human Life, 1995), no. 50.

12. For a brief treatment of these major dimensions of human existence, see Billy, *Evangelical Kernels*, 170–73. For an alternative presentation, see the seven "anthropological constants" developed in Edward Schillebeeckx, *Christ: The Experience of Jesus as Lord* (New York: Crossroad, 1981), 734–43.

13. For a description of the "spirituality of communion," see John Paul II, *Novo millennio ineunte*, nos. 43–45.

14. Even the execution of an act that protects the life of an innocent (a traditional moral absolute in Catholic moral doctrine) must be *personally appropriated* as true and cannot simply be embraced because of its moral absolute status in Catholic doctrine. John Paul II condemns blind obedience in the moral realm as not worthy of human dignity. All moral actions must be executed as "prompted personally from within" (*Veritatis Splendor*, n. 42).

15. Romanus Cessario, *Introduction to Moral Theology* (Washington, DC: The Catholic University of America Press, 2001), 22.

16. Mark Graham, *Josef Fuchs on Natural Law* (Washington, DC: Georgetown University Press, 2002), 230.

17. See a comprehensive account of holiness in the book *Holiness: Past and Present*, ed. Stephen Barton (London: T&T Clark, 2003), 338.

Conclusion

1. Mark McIntosh, *Mystical Theology* (Oxford: Blackwell, 1998), 75.

2. See his spiritual autobiography, which has this sentiment as its major theme: *A Journey with God in Time* (Notre Dame, IN: University of Notre Dame Press, 2003).